Praise for THE ANTI-RACIST WRITING WORKSHOP

"This book is fire. This book is a devotion. With personal anecdotes and memories, with brilliant readings of spaces, classrooms, and texts, Felicia Rose Chavez communicates so much of what is truly at stake in the classroom: our voices, our histories, and our capacities to live ethically, curiously, and in true and deep connection with ourselves and others. I think of June Jordan whose work and legacy swirls all through here: 'It is always the love that will carry action into positive new places, that will carry your own nights and days beyond demoralization and away from suicide.' With that same sense of seriousness and fierce love, Chavez stun~' ɔrients readers toward the ongoing and vital study ·· nd be in together if we commit to this ~· ҽous dismantling just as it is an ur ıes-tions. My heart is so alive reaɑ

—ARACELIS ᵗ _ʋck *Maria*

"'How does one write but not neᵗ ., ɩearn voice?' This is one of the most halting and necessary questions Felicia Rose Chavez poses in *The Anti-Racist Writing Workshop*. What Chavez presents from her experience as workshop participant, artist, activist, and professor is vital and generous. She expertly outlines the steps to produce a nurturing, collaborative, inclusive space for BIPOC writers where the core tenets are about emotional recognition, writing rituals, representative reading lists, and fully collaborative workshops where no one is silenced. *The Anti-Racist Writing Workshop* breaks down how a universal acclamation to inherently racist practices in workshops has stifled and harmed students of color. Chavez shares a methodology that is pure, enlightened, encouraging, and productive, allowing creators of color to understand their value and potential. As an author, editor, and teacher I found myself wholly changed by *The Anti-Racist Writing Workshop* and will be implementing much of this thinking and these actions to facilitate more accountability and unity within the workshop environment."

—JENNIFER BAKER, editor of *Everyday People: The Color of Life—A Short Story Anthology*

"There is power in the words we write. Understanding how we can use those words to build community, challenge racism, and decolonize classrooms is the work of anti-racist educators. Felicia Rose Chavez has skillfully and lovingly done all three in a book that will transform how we write to create an anti-racist world. The writing rituals, questions to push anti-racist thinking, and explanation on how we complete the literary canon will leave the reader with the necessary tools to become a teacher who is building a new world. Chavez lays out powerful and inclusive ways to model a writing workshop structure that would make June Jordan proud."

—DR. BETTINA L. LOVE, author of
We Want to Do More Than Survive

"Part memoir, part pedagogical tract, part guidebook, part testimony, *The Anti-Racist Writing Workshop: How to Decolonize the Creative Classroom* is everything. 'Dismantle' has become a trendy word in our current historical moment. We use it, but don't really know how to dismantle. Felicia Rose Chavez personifies the word. True to the adage, she shows us, doesn't tell us. When it comes to anti-racist pedagogy, most instructors go silent after acknowleging that systemic oppression exists in classrooms worldwide. They go silent as a form of denial, resistance, or they need the how-to, the step-by-step instructions and tools to work with. Chavez brilliantly confronts our comfort levels and our played out forms of teaching. *The Anti-Racist Writing Workshop* is a vital book. If we are truly going to learn, write, and read in an equitable, supportive, creative, humanity-driven environment that seeks to replace white-centered, patriarchal teaching techniques, this book is required reading. It's bound to be an instant classic. Word to everything I love."

—WILLIE PERDOMO, author of *The Crazy Bunch*

"Felicia Chavez's *The Anti-Racist Writing Workshop* is a generational intervention. Chavez is expanding expectations of how-to books while giving radical generative portals of entry into workshop reconstruction. Every writing teacher on Earth needs this book."

—KIESE LAYMON, author of *Heavy*

"*The Anti-Racist Writing Workshop* is an intelligent and necessary rethinking of the creative writing workshop. It provides a map to diversify the workshop and its aesthetics, to restructure its power dynamics, and to align the process of critique more with basic principles of creativity and psychology. We're in a profound cultural and political shift now around race, and Felicia Rose Chavez's book will aid others on that path.

—DAVID MURA, author of *A Stranger's Journey*

ABOUT THE BREAKBEAT POETS SERIES

The BreakBeat Poets series, created by Kevin Coval and Nate Marshall, is committed to work that brings the aesthetic of hip-hop practice to the page. These books are a cipher for the fresh, with an eye always to the next. We strive to center and showcase some of the most exciting voices in literature, art, and culture.

THE BREAKBEAT POETS EDITORIAL BOARD

Cofounders Kevin Coval (Creative Director) and Nate Marshall (Series Editor), Maya Marshall (Managing Editor), Safia Elhillo, Idris Goodwin, and José Olivarez

BREAKBEAT POETS SERIES TITLES INCLUDE

The BreakBeat Poets Vol. 1: New American Poetry in the Age of Hip-Hop,
    edited by Kevin Coval, Quraysh Ali Lansana, and Nate Marshall
This is Modern Art: A Play, Idris Goodwin and Kevin Coval
The BreakBeat Poets Vol. 2: Black Girl Magic, edited by
    Mahogany L. Browne, Jamila Woods, and Idrissa Simmonds
Human Highlight, Idris Goodwin and Kevin Coval
On My Way to Liberation, H. Melt
Black Queer Hoe, Britteney Black Rose Kapri
Citizen Illegal, José Olivarez
Graphite, Patricia Frazier
The BreakBeat Poets Vol. 3: Halal If You Hear Me,
    edited by Fatimah Asghar and Safia Elhillo
Commando, E'mon Lauren
Build Yourself a Boat, Camonghne Felix
Milwaukee Avenue, Kevin Coval
Bloodstone Cowboy, Kara Jackson
Everything Must Go, Kevin Coval, illustrated by Langston Allston
Can I Kick It?, Idris Goodwin
The BreakBeat Poets Vol. 4: LatiNEXT,
    edited by Felicia Rose Chavez, José Olivarez, and Willie Perdomo
Too Much Midnight, by Krista Franklin
Lineage of Rain, Janel Pineda
Milagro, Penelope Allegria
Mama Phife Represents, Cheryl Boyce-Taylor

THE ANTI–RACIST RACIST WRITING WORKSHOP

How to Decolonize the Creative Classroom

Felicia Rose Chavez

Haymarket Books
Chicago, Illinois

© 2021 Felicia Rose Chavez

Published in 2021 by
Haymarket Books
P.O. Box 180165
Chicago, IL 60618
773-583-7884
www.haymarketbooks.org
info@haymarketbooks.org

ISBN: 978-1-64259-267-2

Distributed to the trade in the US through Consortium Book
Sales and Distribution (www.cbsd.com) and internationally
through Ingram Publisher Services International
(www.ingramcontent.com).

This book was published with the generous support of Lannan
Foundation and Wallace Action Fund.

Special discounts are available for bulk purchases by
organizations and institutions. Please call 773-583-7884 or
e-mail info@haymarketbooks.org for more information.

Cover design by Rachel Cohen.

Printed in Canada by union labor.

Library of Congress Cataloging-in-Publication data is available.

4 6 8 10 9 7 5

To Dad, for the poetry, and Mom, for the voice

It did/does seem that there really are ways to change school so that you can get out of it more alive than dead!

—June Jordan, *June Jordan Poetry for the People: A Revolutionary Blueprint*

CONTENTS

PREFACE

A t twenty three years old, I borrowed a beat-up copy of *June Jordan's Poetry for the People: A Revolutionary Blueprint* from the Young Chicago Authors' Writing Teachers Collective. I read it on buses, on trains, carried it in my corduroy messenger bag knowing full well it was stolen goods. How could I give it back? The book revealed me to myself like a treasure map.

Part testament, part movement, June Jordan describes her journey as educator in arresting, no-bullshit poeticism. I felt seen. More accurately, I saw myself in her: a woman of color attempting a different, better, approach to the writing workshop. She said what I felt and *damn* did that matter, because I could stop apologizing for my hurt, could stop apologizing for my anger, could stop wasting my resources on "the way it's always been done" and instead act toward change.

Jordan writes, "As a teacher I was learning how not to hate school: how to overcome the fixed, predetermined, graveyard nature of so much of formal education: come and be buried here among these other (allegedly) honorable dead."[1]

What I remember most is that word, "hate." I sat long hours with that word. I didn't know then that I hated school, only that school hated me, so much so that I bent my brown body into a bow to appease it. I broke out in hives, in tears, because I couldn't yet differentiate my love of learning from the hatred of a white supremacist educational system.

Now, here were June Jordan and her University of California, Berkeley, poetry students teaching me how to cultivate empowerment in my own classroom. "At last," Jordan writes, "you could love school because school did not have to be something apart from, or in denial of, your own life and the multifarious new lives of your heterogeneous students! School could become, in fact, a place where students learned about the world and then resolved, collectively and creatively, to change it!"[2]

Fourteen years later, I presented an early draft of *The Anti-Racist Writing Workshop* to a group of creative writing professors from liberal arts institutions across the country. After the reading, a woman in the audience embraced me in a hug. "You may have just kept me from quitting my job," she whispered, crying. "I was in June Jordan's collective, you know. I needed to remember."

I needed to remember, too, which is why I wrote this book. Here is my own testament, my own movement, a blueprint for a twenty-first-century writing workshop that concedes the humanity of people of color so that we may raise our voices in vote for love over hate.[3]

Decolonizing
the Creative Classroom

A Legacy of Dominance and Control

In graduate school at the University of Iowa's Nonfiction Writing Workshop, I was what you might call a difficult student. I own that. Black hoody, black boots, black coat, slumped in down at the classroom desk. Alert and vocal and pissed off. Alienated and isolated and deeply lonely. And cold! I remember icicles daggering the air, a cold so bad my toilet water froze.

"How quaint," many said about Iowa City. Liberal, walkable, cheap; a real writer's paradise. But I got long stares at the co-op grocery that said "You don't belong here." I was a brown-skinned Chicana, conspicuous in my white picket rental. And when I'd complain about the Iowans who asked me to see them to a fitting room, to refill their water, to point them to a restroom—"I don't work here!" I'd repeat through gritted teeth—my family would tell me to hold my tongue and focus on the writing. I was, after all, lucky to be in the workshop.

Thus the implicit imperative for people of color in MFA programs: to write, but not to exercise voice. Because if we spoke up (if we spoke up!) the Great and Terrible Oz would reveal itself as a sickly white monolith, leaching on tradition in an effort to sustain its self-important power. Still, we were the chosen few, lucky to be there. We were not about to mess it up by complaining, except maybe to one another behind locked doors.

Silencing writers is central to the traditional writing workshop model. Harkening back to 1936, when the University of Iowa instituted the first degree-granting creative writing program in the country, the traditional model mandates that participants read a classmate's manuscript independently, in advance of workshop. Participants proceed to mark up the manuscript, then type a critical response to the writer in letter format. When participants reconvene in workshop, they air their opinions amongst themselves for as long as an hour while the writer takes notes. Per the pedagogical rite of passage, the writer is forbidden to speak. This silencing, particularly of writers of color, is especially destructive in institutions that routinely disregard the lived experiences of people who are not white.

This matrix of silence is so profound it enlists writers of color to eradicate ourselves. Even now, as I type this, my heart tells me "No, you can't say that, you might derail your teaching career, shrink your literary network, hurt their feelings, sound ungrateful, blow things out of proportion." Even though I am the commander of my own experience, my heart tells me to choose subservience out of fear that my narrative might ricochet off of institutionalized white power and smack me upside the head. That's how racism works, right? It's systematic oppression that breeds behavioral norms.

Because when the flowering trees bloomed pink, Iowa City was charming. I'd buy eggrolls and coffee at the farmers market and then spend hours perusing secondhand stores, my fingertips a dusty black, snatching anything colorful to make my house a home. I had friends, a select few brilliant women who dragged me on walks when I'd rather brood, who fed me vegetables when I'd rather binge, who discussed global politics when I lacked perspective. I had earnest students who were unafraid of risk and a champion thesis advisor who reserved me a seat at her family's dinner table. But this book is not about individuals. It's not even about Iowa. Before the University of Iowa, I went to the University of New Mexico, and before that DePaul University and Wellesley College, each of which replicated an identical workshop model.

No, this book is about institutions. More specifically, institutional racism—the system of advantage based on race.

When I speak of the traditional writing workshop model, I speak of an institution of dominance and control upheld by supposedly venerable workshop leaders (primarily white), majority white workshop participants, and canonical white authors memorialized in hefty anthologies, the required texts of study. And when I speak of dominance and control, I'm really talking about silence. I'm not just referring to the traditional workshop ritual of silencing the author when critiquing their work ("building tough skin," they call it, to better prepare for the "real world," as though writers of color live anywhere else, as though our skin is not leathered to the touch), but a profound, ubiquitous silence: the nearly complete omission of writers of color in person and print. It is as though we do not exist.

Junot Díaz puts it well: "I was a person of color in a workshop whose theory of reality did not include my most fundamental experiences as a person of color—that did not, in other words, include me."[1] Here I quote the concrete and systematic issues addressed in Díaz's groundbreaking New Yorker article, while acknowledging his toxic legacy of abuse against women. No doubt Sandra Cisneros puts it better: "I hated it."[2] Díaz is a Pulitzer Prize-winning novelist, Cisneros a MacArthur Fellow; the resentment felt by writers of color is not due to lack of talent—that we can't hang with the big boys—but rather due to the endemic oppression within literary arts programs. This was true when I was a financially independent, first-generation undergraduate student. This was true when I was a graduate fellowship student, and it's true now that I am a Visiting Assistant Professor of English at a private liberal arts college.

It's like writing programs are stuck in 1936, encased in shatterproof glass, museum relics safeguarding whiteness as the essence of literary integrity. In 2018, I was one of the only people of color in my English Department, and that made me feel physically, emotionally, and intellectually at risk for harm. Compound race, gender, and stature ("I thought you were a student!" colleagues would often comment) with my working-class background, and presto: instant and incessant anxiety, catapulting me back in time to when I was a graduate student.

Anxiety when the editor of the literary journal asks me to step down as a volunteer reader because I express concern that her all-white staff might result in aesthetic bias.

Anxiety when a white female professor uses a black pen to cross out references to ethnicity in my personal essay, noting in the margins, "You don't need to make it a race thing."

Anxiety when a white male professor, former Teacher of the Year, keeps me after class to discuss my repeated requests for a more inclusive reading list. He sits inappropriately close, sarcastically mocking how unfair it is, how unfair that I'm not represented in the syllabus. He yells so loud that a concerned colleague knocks on the classroom door (at least that's what she tells me later; between his yelling and my crying, neither of us hear her).

Anxiety when a white male professor, whom I intend to claim as mentor, begins class with a vote. "One of the faculty members"—I'll later learn that it's the administrative assistant rather than one of the seven white nonfiction professors—"insists that we hire a person of color for the Visiting Writers Series. Would you prefer that we bring in a person of color, or a quality writer, someone who's doing really exciting things?"

He suggests that we go around the room, one by one, and voice our vote aloud. I'm the only person of color present, planted at the tail end of the circle, and so I witness twelve or so of my white peers—esteemed journalists and rhetoric instructors alike—play into the false binary: "No, no people of color! We want quality writers only." My whole body shakes like I'm cold, but I'm not cold, I'm hot. "My face must be so red," I remember thinking. "Can't they see my face?" But, of course, they don't see me. That's the point.

That's the motherfucking point.

When it's my turn to vote, I stand up (shaking, hot, my legs disobedient anchors) and exit the room. I don't say a word. I save it for when the garage door shuts behind me at home.

"Why didn't you say anything?" I sometimes ask myself. It was on me to speak for a whole people, and in that moment, I choked. To speak up was to enact my powerlessness, isolating me from my classmates who would go on to befriend one another, marry one another, hire one another later in their careers. To speak up was to square off with my professor, the white person in power, the very man who had attracted me to Iowa, whose favor I courted. The implications, the outcomes of moments like these, can last a lifetime.

Days later, this professor will invite me out for coffee. I'll recount my discomfort in defense of my early exit. "I hardly think I said it like that," he'll reply, rolling his eyes, and an instant trifecta of thoughts will dash the line: one, that I'm just another overexcited brown person, embarrassing myself with wild stories because "come on, it wasn't that bad, can't you just let it go?"; two, that it always comes down to words for us writers, there's power there and we know it; and three, that he's just another calculating white person, attempting to manipulate my narrative to better reflect on him.

One after another, my professors will reach out in attempt to manage "the situation" (the situation being me, of course, and not insatiable white supremacy). I'll endure each awkward exchange—cryptic, self-serving e-mails and hallway chats—and then tick that professor off of my list of potential mentors. In class, my peers are starry-eyed, but I'll have X-ray glasses that expose my professors' bias. Whenever we interact, I'll feel anxious and resentful and vulnerable and regretful, too, that I can't just be cool. I didn't know it then, but I would eventually tick, tick, tick out of options and have to venture outside of the English Department, to Studio Art and Education, in order to secure mentorship.

Oh, to drop out of school, that Everlasting Gobstopper of a fantasy I lodged in my mouth day and night for three years of graduate study. But loyal to my family's wishes, I held my tongue. Or at least the Chicana version of holding my tongue, which was to make a big fuss trying to change the workshop from within. All I had to do was expose the privileged, white, male identity Iowa assumed as universal, right?

Together with a trusted friend from my cohort, I formed a student diversity committee. I served as the elected student liaison to faculty. I petitioned for the "emergency hire" of a professor of color. And I cofounded "Toward a New Canon," an elective class that featured contemporary writers of color.

I channeled my anger into action, and still a white peer called me "militant," another white peer called me "radical," another white peer suggested, over coffee, that I "toe the line until graduation," because "everyone's already stressed out enough."

Here I thought I was a step closer to belonging, if not at the co-op grocery then at least within my own cohort. But no. The backlash was just as hostile as the censorship. Even white allies warned me to "tone it down," fearful that my activism was annihilating my professional network; I was losing the game of graduate school. "Move on," they said, but I wouldn't. And I couldn't. Move where? I wanted to ask. I live in this skin.

I comforted myself with a make-believe Fellowship Girl, how years from now she could exist on the page, maybe write about home—her culture, her birthplace, her body—without suffering the white-splaining workshop critique. Or maybe she could live in her imagination, without pressure to personify her ethnicity. This and more, but only if I succeeded in effecting change.

Around year two, I noticed that my classmates' heads were full of manuscripts, but I was gummed up in diversity's gear-work. My double consciousness had triggered a double burden; between diversity committee meetings, faculty meetings, class meetings, and the inevitable bouts of pissed-off crying, when was I supposed to write? My professors expected me to accommodate their ignorance, explaining racism as though it were an objective subject, separate from themselves. Their impatience and defensiveness got to be too much. "I'm not supposed to be educating you!" I wanted to scream. "I'm supposed to focus on writing."

Over time, even writing proved problematic, for what was I supposed to write about? Certainly not me. To willingly exacerbate the paternalism of my professors and peers by writing memoir, that was just foolish. The genre was, by default, white. My cultural, intellectual, historical, and political consciousness baffled others at best; at worst my writing made them feel left out or guilty or indignant.

I had to be real with myself. All this work, and nothing had changed. Nothing was ever going to change, because the powers that be didn't want change.

Eating pizza in bed started to look a whole lot better than effecting change. I bought a Snuggie. My critical essays were illogical, muddled, my workshop feedback to peers was limp praise, handwritten in the half hour before deadline. Most of all I dreaded my own workshops. Bowing silently while my professor and peers—the ones who wanted quality writers only, the ones who wanted me to toe the line—schooled me in how to write like them. "Use our words," they seemed to say, and "with time and hard work, you, too, can have voice."

I hated it, but I did it, because I was more than just a writer. I was a teacher. I knew that a better workshop model existed because I had conducted one in my own high school creative writing classrooms back in Chicago. My anti-racist approach decentered whiteness and redistributed power equitably among participants and instructors.[3] While I didn't have a graduate cohort to which I belonged and felt safe, at least I could create it for my undergraduate students in Iowa. With adjustments for individual specialization, institutional culture, and legislative standardization, I discovered that the anti-racist workshop model is applicable across the higher education spectrum, from high school to college to graduate school. Everyone benefits from an inclusive approach.

The anti-racist workshop is a study in love. It advances humility and empathy over control and domination, freeing educators to:

» Deconstruct bias to achieve a cultural shift in perspective.

» Design democratic learning spaces for creative concentration.

» Recruit, nourish, and fortify students of color to best empower them to exercise voice.

» Embolden every student to self-advocate as a responsible citizen in a globalized community.

At Iowa I earned an MFA in writing, but it was actually the art of creating healthy, sustainable, and empowering communities in my undergraduate classrooms that I learned over those three years.

At first, I was nervous to institute the alternative, anti-racist workshop model I'd tested in Chicago because my Iowa students were all white. "Would they care?" I wondered. It turns out they did care, so much so that they nominated me for a teaching award. "She encouraged a present-ness in each of us, not only as classmates, but also as human beings, as fellow artists," wrote one student in his nomination letter. Another young woman wrote, "The writing we were introduced to was exciting and playful, new and edgy, with work by people of color and the LGBTQ community, which you never find in English class. It was truly 'hands-on' education, thinking critically about what we read and saw from contemporary artists." I won the award, but more so, I won the confidence to formalize my workshop into a replicable model, one that I've honed in large and small groups across the country. *The Anti-Racist Writing Workshop* is the culmination of thirteen years of progressive educational practice, a synthesis of my most successful teaching strategies.

The Traditional Model vs. the Anti-Racist Model at a Glance

Let's break down how the anti-racist workshop model consciously works against traditions of dominance in the creative classroom:

The traditional model honors predominately white workshop leaders renowned for their high-caliber publications and degree accreditation.	The anti-racist model honors workshop leaders who've earned distinction as innovative and effective allies to writers of color, ranking superior teaching over publication credits or master's awards.
The traditional model bestows a select few scholarships to exceptional writers of color, ensuring a placeholder for "diversity" in otherwise all-white writing classrooms.	The anti-racist model actively recruits people of color to participate in writing workshops regardless of whether they identify as creative, reiterating that their experiences are crucial to our collective narrative.
The traditional model affirms the authority of white literary "masters" through a strict study of canonical texts, imparting an implicit rubric for the "right" way to write.	The anti-racist model surveys a living archive of scanned print material and multimedia art by a range of writers including people of color, differently abled writers, and people who are LGBTQIA2+. These texts are sourced by students and instructors over the course of the term, acknowledging that craft, form, and content are multidimensional and malleable.
The traditional model traps text on the page, asking workshop participants to impose their individual interpretations of the story's meaning.	The anti-racist model pairs an assigned text with a conversation with the author, contextualizing their stories within a specific lived experience, making meaning relevant and real.

The traditional model assumes that workshop participants share an identical knowledge of craft, and wields academic vocabulary as a badge of authority.	The anti-racist model confirms craft as an abstract concept; participants collectively define the workshop vocabulary.
The traditional model silences the author during workshop while participants compete over what's "right" and "wrong" with the text.	The anti-racist model empowers the author to moderate their own workshop while participants rally in service of the author's vision.
The traditional model exalts the workshop leader as the dominant opinion; they write on the author's text with the expectation that the author will revise comment by comment.	The anti-racist model distinguishes the workshop leader as artistic ally; they engage in one-on-one conferences with the author before and after workshop, dialoguing about how to best achieve the author's vision.

If we are to evolve the traditional workshop model into an enlightened, democratic counterculture, then we must concede the obvious: that writers of color exist. No more of this obsolete white supremacist aesthetic! It is time to admit that writing is a political, historical, and ideological act steeped in identity politics. It's an essential act, an urgent act, an act that has cultivated critical mass since the traditional writing workshop model was first developed.

It's time to take stock. Eight decades, we've clung to this model, and where are we now? In her *Rumpus* article "Where Things Stand," Roxane Gay calculates that as of 2012, full-time professors were nearly 90 percent white. The publishing industry was nearly 90 percent white. And the books reviewed in the *New York Times* were written by nearly 90 percent white authors.[4] That's dominance. That's control. That's the silencing of nonwhite authors.

The gaping need for creative revolution is real. It's time to demand better not just for writers of color in our own separate art collectives but for everyone, everywhere. Organizations like VONA, Macando, CantoMundo, Cave Canem, Watering Hole, Lambda Literary, Kundiman, and the Asian American Writers' Workshop are indispensable to our collective arts culture, fortifying and revitalizing the psyches of countless writers of color across the country. It is because of the essential work of torchbearers like Sandra Cisneros that I am emboldened to propose that all writers deserve a safe space for creative concentration and exposure to the literary traditions of writers of color. Consider every one of us deprived. Were we to stop worshiping whiteness as default and adjust the parallax to include racialized bodies, we'd reveal whole continents of complexity to enrich our literary integrity.

The time for change is now. We can't wait it out in hopes of a better tomorrow, because today's creative writing cohort hires tomorrow's teachers, edits tomorrow's magazines, produces tomorrow's plays, and acquires tomorrow's manuscripts. Their investigative journalism can incite tomorrow's impeachment; their stump speech can secure tomorrow's seat in public office. What may read as a crisis in creative writing is at heart a crisis in American culture: without voice, participatory democracy fails.

To claim a public voice is to summon our collective power, belly-deep and then bitter in our throats, a willful insistence that we matter—and we do matter, especially now, in the twenty-first-century United States of America, with a president who hates us, an economy that exploits us, a police force that murders us, a culture that embezzles from us only to elicit our shame, our silence; we write to drown out the silence.

So let's get writing. But not on their terms. On ours.

How to Use This Book

The blueprint's all laid out for you, here. Each chapter of this book walks step-by-step through the fundamentals of protecting and platforming writers of color, offering replicable reading, writing, workshop, critique, and assessment strategies. Apply the lot or pick and choose, individualizing a model that best serves your vision:

Chapter 1: Preparing for Change

We begin by tackling student recruitment. Too often writers of color conclude that workshops are hazardous because they're not represented among the faculty, they're not represented in the syllabus, and they're not represented within the class cohort. Chapter 1 offers an appraisal of our workshop marketing materials and syllabi in a targeted effort to enlist more writers of color.

Chapter 2: Fostering Engagement, Mindfulness, and Generosity

Chapter 2 guarantees our writers of color remain enrolled, pairing creative writing exercises with personalized check-ins and freewriting exercises to unmask the psychological, emotional, and cultural barriers to creative expression. Participants name their fears and then write past them, promoting a collective sense of power.

Chapter 3: Instituting Reading and Writing Rituals

We then transition into how to read creative writing, not as an inert receptacle for our opinions but as an instrument of authorial choice. Chapter 3 launches a multi-step reading ritual, beginning first with workshop participants' own words—handwritten, raw, and messy—read aloud to the group. By prioritizing workshop participants' writing over model canonical texts, we celebrate students' own words, spoken aloud in their unique and powerful voices, versus an artificial imitation of white literary "masters."

Chapter 4: Completing the Canon

Gradually, we transition into reading contemporary writers from a living archive that features people of color, women, queer, differently abled, and gender-nonconforming artists. The final step is for participants to engage in educated exchanges with one or more published authors, contextualizing a text within a specific lived experience. Workshop participants see themselves reflected in these professionals, empowering them to claim the identity of author.

Chapter 5: Owning the Language of Craft

Chapter 5 demands that all workshop participants have equal access to the language of craft. The traditional workshop model is rife with assumed knowledge, lobbing vocabulary such as voice, imagery, characterization, and arrangement in discussion as though it were common know-how. When we make these abstract ideas concrete, we empower participants to proactively define a lexicon of craft elements with which to discuss one another's work.

Chapter 6: Teaching Writers to Workshop

Next, we learn how to workshop, an intricate skill that traditional leaders habitually undervalue. Participants read their texts aloud and moderate their own feedback sessions. This artist-centered model, inspired by Liz Lerman's Critical Response Process, trains participants in how to check their egos, exercise kinship, and read in service of the author's agenda.

Chapter 7: Conferencing as Critique

Chapter 7 advises us to put the red pen in the writer's hand. Instead of scribbling on participants' work, prescribing alternate grammar, phrasing, or narrative strategies that align with our personal aesthetic preferences, consider verbal critique. Guided pre- and post-workshop conferences in which the writer marks on their own work allows us to dialogue with participants instead of dominate over them.

Chapter 8: Promoting Camaraderie and Collective Power

We round out the book with assessment strategies, squashing labels of "good" or "bad" in an effort to move beyond hierarchy. Chapter 8 evaluates participants' real learning beyond a rote implementation of the workshop leader's critique or placement in a competitive showcase of the "best" writing, opting instead for individual, process-based assessment. Rather than outward, workshop participants go inward with perspective and intention to gauge their personal progress.

Appendix 1: Platforming Writers of Color: A Twenty-First-Century Reference Guide

The book culminates with a twenty-first-century reference guide of contemporary writers of color and progressive publishing platforms to help dispel the myth of scarcity that there simply are not enough quality writers of color out there.

Appendix 2: Platforming Writers of Color: A Twenty-First-Century Reference Guide

For further reference, Appendix 2 provides sample lesson plans for educators who seek out the logistics of an anti-racist workshop agenda in action.

It's time we shift toward evolution. As opposed to an exercise in ego, the anti-racist workshop model teaches engagement, mindfulness, and generosity. No talking over, no talking down to, no muzzling writers of color.

Everything you need to decolonize your creative classroom, to ratify the future of education, is within your grasp. Instead of trapping yourself eighty years in the past, project eighty years into the future: What do you want tomorrow's creative writing workshop to look like?

The Future of Creative Writing

Let's not get it twisted: this anti-racist writing pedagogy is aggressive activism. It's immediate, tangible action that disrupts the legacy of white supremacy by changing organizational structures, policies, practices, and attitudes, so that power is redistributed and shared equitably.

Folks whom you respect and trust might say this model sounds excessive. That it disservices writers of color by coddling them. That it's soft, feminine, or naive. That it unfairly advantages "inferior" writers of color over their white peers. That it's a symptom of affirmative action, a bunch of ethnic studies propaganda, typical of our spoiled, spineless, politically correct generation. That it's reverse racism, or—astonishingly!—that it's redundant, because "racism no longer exists."

The bewilderment, the resistance, the hostility may be all too familiar. Just nod and carry on: you hear them; but our young people of color deserve priority.

My own students occasionally express opposition to the antiracist workshop model. They'll request a one-on-one conference, only to complain that their peers are "too nice." They want instead for their classmates to "be real," to "be harsh," to "tear the work apart" because they can "take it."

These students, in my experience, are always privileged white males. Every single time.

And while my sampling pool might be skewed (I teach at a prestigious private college in Colorado), I believe there's something to learn from the pushback of white male students. They want to compete in workshop. Or, more accurately, they want to win workshop. Without acknowledging, of course, that the game is rigged, that they won at the get-go, regardless of their writing ability. This colosseum mentality of brutality and bloodshed is a farce, one that blinds them to the advantage of collaborative creation.

In conference, I suggest that the students focus less on the workshop critique they receive and more on the prompts they provide. Did they ask pointed questions to elicit specific, insightful feedback, or were they passive, vague, sacrificial storytellers awaiting the knife? "Is it any good?" these white male students tend to ask, well accustomed to instantaneous response (their lawyer grandfather, their novelist father, their editor mother, their uncle's old golfing buddy, admissions director to dream school). Confident in their place in the world, their effortless access to attentive ears, they balk at politeness as though it were backward: "I don't want to be spoken to that way; I want callousness, the 'Truth.'"

Unlike their peers of color, their lives do not depend on civility and cooperation. "Can't we all just speak our minds?" is the unknowable privilege of white people. It's a clever invitation, a sly smile, a loaded gun. Because say the "wrong" thing—and I have, when enforcing my course policies regarding attendance, participation, or deadlines—and BOOM, their fathers fire patronizing e-mails about what their sons deserve. Not what they've earned, but what they deserve. And just like that, the game of being "real," of "taking it," is over.

With time, these white male students acquiesce to the anti-racist model—the transformation is truly rewarding—but as is the trend with apple barrels, there's usually one who remains disgruntled. Just this past fall, I remember a writer of color who cried during check-in (a daily ritual to begin workshop, referenced in chapter 2). She said that she had a "rough night," to which a white male student responded with a theatrical sigh. After class, in my office, he complained that it's "annoying" to sit through check-in, because what could have possibly happened between yesterday and today? What, indeed.

As an undergraduate English major at DePaul University, I crisscrossed the city of Chicago, tutoring wealthy white children in their pristine homes. It was a well-paying, massive exercise in self-effacement, one I've rarely spoken about out of shame, for the reality of "private writing tutor" so drastically contrasted the line on my résumé. White fathers sometimes fingered my hair or grazed my breast before handing me my paycheck; white mothers often expressed exasperation when I refused to cook or clean. "I'll pay extra!" they'd relent, misreading my rejection as barter. I was the brown nonperson, hired help, deferring my own college coursework in order to write their children's five-paragraph essays.

All this to afford my tuition, rent, utilities, toiletries, groceries, clothes, bus fare, plane fare, and also stamps, to mail whatever money was left over to my parents, both of whom collected disability. It wasn't always so—my parents kicked off careers in the service industry while they were in middle school—but during the course of my undergraduate study, my dad suffered physical pain, my mom emotional.

I strategically timed that daily phone call home to Albuquerque until after my homework was done.

A conversation with my mom, especially, could derail me for hours, the late-night agony of should I stay in school, or go back home where I'm needed? A good Chicana should be by her mother's side. I didn't need some fancy school to teach me that.

On the phone, my parents and I never spoke of my own pain: the impossible divide between my classmates and I, that racial and socioeconomic gulf I internalized each time I arrived on campus. Friendless, I'd trail behind groups of orange-skinned girls in North Face fleece. They'd turn left, toward the dorms (warm meals served up on trays, care packages from mom, late-night roommate confessionals), and I'd turn right, toward the train and then the bus, back to my too-cold studio apartment. I was so goddamn lonely, frozen in my thrift-store jacket, exhausted from teaching other people's children, guilty at my own greedy desire for education, and spitfire angry that nothing ever came easy.

So yeah, a lot can happen between one day and the next. If a professor had just once taken time out of class to ask me how I was doing, I, too, might have cried. I, too, might have said, "I had a rough night."

If we're aiming for Truth, young men, then here it is: I'm at peace with the occasional white workshop participant's discomfort, because it's evidence that the anti-racist model is working. For the first time in their artistic careers, white writers must listen—to multidimensional storytelling, to marginalized narratives, to the anxieties and aspirations of their peers—without a single appeal for their opinion. Listening is the first and most important step for maintaining a storytelling tradition, and as such, we must practice it daily. Writers of color are accustomed to this practice, burdened with ears so elastic we're capable of hearing multiple, simultaneous subtexts in every exchange.

At heart, *The Anti-Racist Writing Workshop* imparts a pedagogy of deep listening. We invest in one another as complex individuals. We confront the voices in our heads that tell us our stories are unimportant. We honor the sidelined narratives of people of color, women, queer, differently abled, and gender-nonconforming artists. We listen to one another's writing, read aloud in workshop, ever conscious of our body language. We ask questions with the intent to understand instead of retort. We read for craft over content, regardless of our subjectivity. And we adhere to the author's agenda during feedback sessions. It requires self-discipline to be sure, but cultivating listening in the creative classroom makes us better writers. We're more present in our lives, better able to articulate what it is to be human. The resulting work rings with vitality.

I'm offering a new approach for a new millennium; it's okay if a few students and colleagues are slow to catch up. Because that young woman who cried during check-in is evidence that the model is working, evidence of her vulnerability and trust, her internal mutiny against the cultural imperative of safety in self-effacement. As Audre Lorde reminds us, "We cannot fight old power in old power terms only. The way we can do it is by creating another whole structure that touches every aspect of our existence, at the same time as we are resisting."[5]

The anti-racist model is working. I've witnessed it, again and again. Workshop participants thank me for making writing relevant and personal; for allowing for freedom of thought; for establishing mutual respect, trust, and agency; for curating a safe, welcoming environment; for hosting a creative community; for tailoring the workshop to who they are as people; for doing their stories justice; for reframing the objective from a product to a state of mind; for inspiring them to look at everything differently, now.

"Felicia feels like the future of education," wrote a young woman in my most recent round of course evaluations. How profoundly I want to honor that sentiment. If only I could time travel, first backward to that young woman in the black hoody, black boots, black coat, slumped in down at the classroom desk—I'd hold her hand, reassure her that she matters, I matter—and then we'd bolt, full-force forward to where we belong, to the future of creative writing, where multicultural consciousness holds weight and substance, where our brown bodies are emboldened to "speak, poet."

What will it look like, sound like? The choice is ours.

CHAPTER ONE

Preparing for Change

First Impressions Matter

When I think of first impressions, I think of Qumbya Housing Co-operative. Kumbya, like the spiritual, only colonizer cute, with a Q. I was nineteen years old, the sort of age when you move to Chicago having never visited, when you apply for a room in a University of Chicago–affiliated co-op despite not being a student. I packed art supplies, an air mattress, and a few dresses into an oversized thrift-store suitcase and made my way from Albuquerque, New Mexico, to Chicago's South Side.

It was the smell that hit me first. I'd later come to identify it as the adventurous approximation of ethnic vegetarian fare, but at the time, the door to Qumbya's three-story brownstone swung open and I inhaled a balmy waft of displacement, that instantaneous understanding that this place was not for people of color. Fifteen white housemates greeted me by the front staircase, their hands hennaed, their hair dreaded, their liberal hubris unchecked. "An Indian princess is among us," announced one of the young men. When I didn't smile, he snapped, "What!? I was being nice." Then he abandoned English altogether, indicating my second-floor bedroom with a prolonged meow.

I didn't have the money to move out, and so I spent my first Chicago year in Qumbya's periphery, slipping in and out of communal spaces overly crowded with caricature: kimonos on Halloween, sombreros on Cinco de Mayo. They had a nickname for me—The Liar—because a detail in my co-op application essay didn't compute, how the desert mountains can be both sun-soaked and snowy. The house culture was calculating, disciplined, with laminated signage on proper sponge use and math problems penned on toilet paper. I didn't add up, and so: The Liar. At the time I laughed, arguing, "No, you've got it all wrong," but who was I kidding? I wasn't even vegetarian.

To avoid house meetings, I'd go to the gym around the corner and sit in the sauna, fully clothed in my coat and boots, until someone complained, or else I'd hang out in the Boston Market across the street, famished for meat. At home, I'd do the minimum expected of me, with the exception of cleaning the second-floor bathroom, which was spotless, everyone said so, egging my anxiety about playing the stereotypical Mexican maid.

I lived in the co-op for a year, taking two buses and two trains from my white household through my Black neighborhood to a Puerto Rican high school, where I taught after-school writing workshops. When my lease was up, the house manager pulled me aside and said, "Listen, I'm sorry, but if you're looking for a letter of rec for another co-op, I can't write it. You were a really bad member."

I summon this memory when a student of color fails an assignment, when a student of color drops a class, when a student of color withdraws from school because they were "bad." Not ostracized, demoralized, exasperated, lonely, or depressed. Just "bad."

Back then, I was indignant, both at the prospect of living in a second co-op—Oh hell no!—as well as the house manager's assumption that I'd ever been a member of the first. I was The Indian Princess, The Liar, The Maid. I was me as seen through their eyes. Membership necessitates mutual participation, but there wasn't vacancy in Qumbya's Cooperative for my authentic self.

"But how did you know," white allies have asked, "that you didn't belong? Was it something someone said, or did?" In other words, wasn't my intuition that "place x is not for people of color" just a prejudicial snap judgement?

The truth is, people of color have been doing this our whole lives, surviving by intuition, navigating spaces safe and unsafe. We knock at a door. The door opens, if we're lucky. And just as quickly, it closes, not because of bruised egos, but because the collective infrastructure is not built to accommodate our bodies, histories, experiences, and opinions. Sometimes the infrastructure reinforces hostility and violence, sometimes it's stares and silence, sometimes it's "colorblind" meritocracy. Other times, like at Qumbya, it's cultural appropriation, free of accountability. White colonialism takes up all the air, so much so that we're forced to step outside to breathe. It doesn't matter if we play-act at home, as many of us do. The fact still remains, we're outside looking in.

Like when teenagers Kanewakeron Thomas Gray and Skanahwati Lloyd Gray tour their dream college of Colorado State University, and campus police sequester and harass them because a white parent felt "they don't belong."[1]

Like when Smith undergraduate Oumou Kanoute eats lunch on break from her on-campus job, and a white staff member summons campus police because the girl "seem[ed] to be out of place."[2]

Like when Yale graduate student Lolade Siyonbola falls asleep in her dorm's common room while working on an essay, and a white student calls campus police to "verify you belong here."[3]

Like when University of Massachusetts–Amherst staff member Reginald Andrade arrives at his office, and campus police search his gym bag, interrogating him about his whereabouts after an anonymous claim that an "agitated African-American" was on the premises.[4]

Like when Emory University professor George Yancy publishes an op-ed about his research on race in the *New York Times*, and receives hundreds of hate messages from white readers calling him "another uppity Nigger."[5]

Membership necessitates mutual participation. How can we possibly achieve membership when our presence—the feat of occupying space in brown skin—is deemed illegitimate? We're nonpeople, exploited for our optics, meant to be seen and not heard. The infrastructure cannot, will not, contain us.

The writing classroom is no exception. English classes, in particular, position people of color as "Other" in order to satisfy a meticulously curated white supremacist agenda: a "classical" education. Kiese Laymon wrestles with the magnitude of racial bias in his early education in *Heavy: An American Memoir*:

> . . . even before I actually met white folk, I met every protagonist, antagonist, and writer of all the stories I ever read in first, second, third, fourth, fifth, sixth, seventh, and eighth grade. At the same time, I met Wonder Woman, the narrator on the *The Wonder Years*, Ricky from Silver Spoons, Booger from *Revenge of the Nerds*, Spock from *Star Trek*, Mallory from *Family Ties*, damn near all the coaches and owners of my favorite teams . . . I met all the Jetsons, all the Flintstones, all the Beverly Hillbillies, the entire Full House, damn near everyone in Pee Wee's Playhouse, all American Presidents, the dudes they said were Jesus and Adam, the women they said were the Virgin Mary and Eve, and all the characters on Grandmama's stories . . . That meant we knew white folk. That meant white folk did not know us.[6]

This is what systematic institutional and cultural racism looks like. By the time people of color hit high school, we're experts on the intricacies of real and imagined whiteness. And yet secondary and post-secondary English classes insist on an in-depth study of "the classics," a learning standard that privileges white narratives and reinforces white superiority. The fact that English Departments so often house creative writing programs proves problematic, for the infrastructure inherently biases workshop curriculum.

People of color know this, which is why so many of us opt out of enrollment. One glance at a creative writing course poster featuring a bust of Shakespeare or a white hand gripping a quill tells us all we need to know about the workshop leaders' allegiances; a Visiting Writers Series flyer featuring majority white authors illustrates an overt devaluing of writers of color; a quick skim of a workshop syllabus with a majority white reading list attests to the oppressive infrastructure in place. These details matter, communicating to participants whether or not our classrooms are safe places for people of color.

First impressions matter.

Anti-racist workshop leaders, ask yourselves, if a person of color were to knock at my workshop door, would it slam shut in their face? This chapter examines the implicit values embedded in our workshop course descriptions and syllabi, with the end goal of recruiting writers of color. A targeted redrafting of our core principles—principles we often fail to see—coupled with the active recruitment of people of color, can result in a multicultural writing collective, one that appeals to writers and non-writers alike. Because whether or not participants identify as creative, their experiences are crucial to our collective narrative.

A Safe Space for Creative Concentration

When people of color receive an invitation to write, to exercise voice in public space, naturally we're wary. Our lives are an exercise in repression—the everyday denial of voice—so as to safeguard our bodies. By not speaking out, we reassure white people that we are inoffensive, nondisruptive, not at all how they see us, be it consciously or subconsciously; that is, as imbeciles, criminals, clowns, or whores. And we deny ourselves voice in order to avoid losing our shit. Because once we open our mouths, who knows what'll come out, and when it'll stop. Our welfare depends on a cultural imperative of silence.

That's why I just come out and say it: "Take my class! I teach an anti-racist writing workshop."

I e-mail this message to student-led organizations and influential faculty members that support people of color, first-generation college students, feminists, activists, and queer and questioning students. The title of my e-mail? "A Safe Space for Creative Concentration." I define "safe" as a student's right to retain their own authority, integrity, and personal artistic preferences throughout the creative writing process without fear of free-reining bigotry.

In the message, I share the story of my past frustrations in workshop, and then counter that narrative with my own approach. Mainly, that I believe that writing is a political act, and in order to honor that offering, we must consciously work against traditions of dominance and control in the creative writing classroom, curating safe spaces for participants to explore race, class, gender, and sexual orientation. Don't worry about being creative, I plead. It's not about that. It's about sharing our stories. We must be heard.

The first time I sent this e-mail, I was nervous as hell. I imagined the collective eye roll of my white colleagues: An anti-racist writing workshop? What does that even mean? It didn't help that I was new to campus. I couldn't rely on reputation to substantiate me. I felt vulnerable, wary of the backlash I might encounter.

But then I got that first response from a student, a quick-fire e-mail in all caps: "YES! I'M IN!" I didn't know this person, had never worked with him before, yet he understood without me even having to explain. At that moment I knew that I was on to something.

I wasn't crazy. It wasn't just me.

People of color need a collaborative artistic community to which they belong and feel safe; they need it, but they don't always know how to ask for it and are often unaware that alternatives exist. It's our responsibility as workshop leaders to verbalize our anti-racist agenda for them, in clear, unapologetic language, language that opens doors instead of closes them. We must reach out to people of color, openly differentiate our approach to the writing workshop, and then welcome them into our collective.

As opposed to the norm—recruiting, exploiting, and then wholly disregarding a few token writers of color in an otherwise all white workshop—the anti-racist approach demands that we dismantle the traditional infrastructure first, and then go about recruitment second.

To recruit writers of color, we've got to be about it.

Being about it isn't easy, because we're forced to articulate our writing workshop principles independent of the old infrastructure. Suddenly the way it's always been done feels like a crutch; without it, we might stumble. That crutch is the "monument of white ide-

ology" of which Claudia Rankine writes in her essay, "
Racism in Creative Writing":

> To maintain our many writing departments with thei
> white faculty has, we often forget, taken conscious work, choice,
> and insistence. The perpetuation of white orientation, white
> narrative, white point of reference, white privilege, white deni-
> al, white dominance, and white defensiveness, if any of these
> things are pointed out or questioned, has taken work and is the
> originating problem.[7]

In other words, maintaining the status quo takes time, energy,
and resources, all of which we claim to lack when it comes to creating an alternative, anti-racist model.

Admitting that neutrality does not exist—that we currently
fuel politicized, race-based writing workshops—is the first and most
important step toward change. To bring down the monument of
white-centered ideology, we've got to dismantle not only the pedagogical infrastructure of white bias, but also the white supremacist
ego of domination and control behind the decision-making.

Where do we even begin?

Let's take a cue from successful course designers and begin at
the end, evaluating the values implicit in our writing workshops'
learning objectives.

Disarming the Master's Tools

What are the goals of your workshop? This is the stuff of course
descriptions, those one-paragraph windows into your classroom.
Harried workshop leaders tend to write course descriptions on
deadline, or better yet, plug in recycled language from hand-me-
down syllabi, with the aim of checking a bureaucratic box more
than conscientiously articulating how participants will transform
under their guidance. Remember that in recruiting people of color
especially, first impressions matter, and that includes your writing
workshop description. It's not enough to desire diversity; you must

plot an anti-racist workshop, differentiating your endgame from the traditional model.

A quick online search (not to mention years of personal experience) reveals that most writing workshop learning objectives tend to be identical. Strip away flourishes, and the boilerplate language reads something like:

Upon completion of this course, participants will

» Engage in the art of literary writing

» Read the master writers in order to develop a fundamental grasp of the genre(s)

» Write through an imitation of the master writers

» Develop a critical vocabulary of craft

» Receive critique via workshop

» Demonstrate improvement in writing

» Study the rules of the English language

This tidy enumeration summarizes the traditional workshop model, in which participants are barren, bereft of storytelling experience and unexposed to learnèd literacy, much less proper English. In effect, traditional workshop leaders reinforce the myth of inferiority.

I mean, they use the word master.

And it flies—of course it flies!—because so many of us are convinced that we're bad at writing, that we aren't creative, that we don't like reading because books are too old and irrelevant.

What if you revised your workshop goals to convince participants that they are experts in their own right? Rather than serve as passive receptacles for white authorship, a democratic educational model demands that all participants contribute to knowledge production. Let's deconstruct the traditional workshop goals in an effort to foster a twenty-first-century anti-racist alternative.

1. Engage in the art of literary writing

The insistence on literary writing is an apt starting place, for what is "literary" code for? A lot of workshop leaders front like even they don't know, appending a jokey "whatever that means" in parentheticals. Because who wants to come out and say it? Literary means civilized, cultured, "classical" writing. (There's that word again! Evidence that English and creative writing share a mutual reinforcement of white supremacist infrastructure.) This is not your common creative expression; it's not genre entertainment for the masses. Literary writing has noble merit, in the tradition of privileged white male figureheads. It's infused with elevated purpose, grappling with complex truths and the profundity of the (privileged, white, male) human condition.

"Literary," in sum, means gatekeeper.

"There seems to be a more or less tacit agreement among literary scholars," writes Toni Morrison in *Playing in the Dark: Whiteness and the Literary Imagination*, "that, because American literature has been clearly the preserve of white male views, genius, and power, those views, genius, and power are without relationship to and removed from the overwhelming presence of black people in the United States." Morrison argues that "this black presence is central to any understanding of our national literature and should not be permitted to hover at the margins of the literary imagination."[8] There is no such thing as white literary purity, no chance at comprehending classical narratives without the political, historical, creative, and cultural contexts of African, Latinx, Native, and Asian Americans. Still, traditional workshop leaders insist on playing gatekeeper, segregating literature and thereby limiting our full artistic realization.

What if you brought down the gate?

Ditching "literary" means ditching an elitist tradition that positions writers of color as outsiders, forced to imitate whiteness in order to earn their badge of literacy. Instead, consider persuading participants that over the course of the workshop, they will succeed in one or more of the following:

» Write in order to achieve their best work

» Manage their ongoing development through regular self-assessment and reflection opportunities

» Pursue creative writing topics of their own choosing

» Experiment with narrative techniques most important to them

» Grow in confidence as writers

Note that in the list above, the workshop leader regards participants as individuals with varying aesthetic preferences. There's a mutual respect at play, a willingness to support participants' personal artistic journeys.

Bottom line: the workshop leader affirms that participants arrive at the classroom as writers, whether or not they know it yet. Each of them comes from a unique storytelling tradition. There's no gauntlet through which they must earn their literacy, only opportunities to enhance their storytelling abilities, both in terms of technical skillset and psychological savvy. It's within this multiplicity of voices that participants fully comprehend the significance of their own story.

True, ditching the term "literary" shrinks the workshop leader's supremacy as art's official gatekeeper. That's a hit to the ego. But student storytelling is not, was not ever, yours to conquer, control, and manipulate to your aesthetic. You are artistic ally, trusted confidant, ready resource, steady guide. Your confidence in their innate ability as writers does wonders to your workshop participants.

2. Read the masters to develop a fundamental grasp of the genre

The masters. Master narratives. "Our" great authors. Writers "we" love. The prevalence of this phrasing reveals creative writing's problematic infrastructure.

What's most disconcerting is that so many workshop leaders refuse to acknowledge it! The imperialist dichotomy of novice/master (and its swift subliminal substitution, slave/master) translates to one who is dependent on, and controlled by, the other; one who is forced into a pretense of obedience in order to maintain self-preservation. And you expect people of color to enroll in your class?

Disarming the master's tools requires first and foremost that we break with colonial legacy and stop using the word master in our syllabi. People of color do not read master as expert. They read it as slave driver. Rapist. Lawmaker barring Black people's right to read, their right to be fully human.

Considering workshop leaders are keen to the nuances of language, I must ask: What purpose does this phrasing serve? A generous me might reason that in order to "engage in the art of literary writing"—a tradition we've established as privileged, white, and male—participants must duly study white male figureheads, those so-called canonical masters of literature, appointed by white people for white people. According to this logic, a close reading of white authors bequeaths novices with a "fundamental grasp" of creative writing principles—principles so superior they simply don't exist elsewhere in print.

A less generous me might reason that the racist language is on point. We don't belong, on purpose.

I remember roaming the campus bookstore as an undergraduate English major. I didn't need course descriptions to determine my schedule, I'd just seek out whichever classes required texts by writers of color. (This system landed me under the tutelage of many purple-haired graduate students, as opposed to tenured professors.) Back then, as now, the shelves hawked T. S. Eliot, Henrik Ibsen, and Mark Twain; Ernest Hemmingway, Jane Austen, and Robert Frost; Joan Didion, Tobias Wolff, and Sam Shepard; Raymond Carver, Flannery O'Connor, and Wallace Stevens; David Mamet, Emily Dickenson, and David Foster Wallace. It's startling as a young person of color to stare down the spines of literacy and note the neat annihilation of most of the world.

Now that I'm the professor, I know that neither my department chair nor my colleagues roam the bookstore tallying writers of color, as I once did. I have free rein to preserve the masters, free rein to impose a white supremacist imperialist dichotomy upon my students.

Unless I choose not to. Unless *you* choose not to.

To be clear: such a choice does not devalue the canon. The canon still commands our reverence. It's the depth of that reverence I call into question. Why the dogged defense of white writers as Western culture's truest and most trusted knowledge set?

I remember a white male colleague's indignation one year when, instead of the usual seminar on Shakespeare, the Theater Department opted for a one-off elective featuring multicultural playwrights. "But it's Shakespeare!" he argued, even after losing the departmental vote. "What will the kids do without Shakespeare?" His outrage, his despair, his stubborn refusal to greenlight a token gesture of plurality, had me shaking my head in wonderment. What was he so afraid of?

This sort of hysterical blindness is commonplace. Denial, fear, revolt, despair, all at the mere suggestion of inclusivity. To supplant master with slave is inconceivable, but that kind of honesty doesn't fly in departmental meetings. It's so much easier to say, "The canon! We must preserve the canon!"

It's your choice.

What if, upon completion of this course, participants:

» Engage in a supportive arts community

» Study one another's writing to enhance their appreciation of the genre(s)

» Select readings from a living archive of multicultural texts that best inform their individual projects

» Curate their own literary anthologies with texts that appeal to their aesthetic preferences

In other words, what if you honored participants' creative integrity, evolving them from novices to equals, writers who share community, kinship, and knowledge? What if you went so far as to count participants' own writing as the required reading, supplemented with contemporary multicultural texts tailored to their taste? What if participants themselves determined the course reading list, disrupting the boundaries between "good" and "bad" art? This is what it is to catapult the workshop into the twenty-first century.

"Sometime around 2040 or sooner, we will no longer be a white majority country," David Mura points out in his essay "Ferguson, Whiteness as Default, and the Teaching of Creative Writing." He writes:

> Artists of color, who are both re-envisioning the past and creating our future, know what it means to be a racial minority in America. This knowledge is embedded within our imaginations and identities, and we speak from that knowledge. That knowledge is out there for white artists to share, but whether they want to avail themselves of that knowledge is another question, one they will have to answer if they are to prepare themselves for the America that is surely coming.[9]

Empower your writers of color to speak from their knowledge. Honor their influences, their imagination, and their intellectual curiosity. By doing so, you enrich your workshop's educational value.

The choice is yours: resuscitate the traditional model of novice/master—a harmful legacy of dependency and obedience that forces people of color to kowtow to archetypal white authorship—or relinquish control and adopt a more profound, dynamic system of study.

3. Write through an imitation of the masters

The best way to learn how to write is through imitation. Workshop leaders love to repeat this refrain. And I get it—reading is essential to a writer's sensibility—but when imitation is applied as a workshop strategy, it's uninspired busywork at best; at worst, it morphs into a problematic power play.

Wielding absolute authority, traditional workshop leaders select and assign white authors for student study (save for the occasional Baldwin, of course). Read this text, absorb it—the topic, structure, style, voice–and then copy it. Prove your literacy by climb-ing inside the master's mouth and parroting whiteness.

Writers of color do not risk workshop–risk exercising voice in public space–to engage in mimicry. We spend our whole lives studying white people and assimilating accordingly. We are experts at performing the rule, and yet we must prove ourselves on the page, too, satisfying the sound of whiteness? Where, when, can we venture to sound like ourselves?

What if the model text is by a person of color, you might ask. Does that enhance the imitation exercise? While exposing workshop participants to texts by writers of color is always a good call, I argue that the pretense of copywork is in and of itself disempowering.

Hating on imitation makes me an outcast, I know. It is the central creative writing teaching tool, one that workshop leaders across the spectrum prize. Still, I've always been baffled by it as an educational model. I call it the search and find, a puzzle that bored me as a kid because the win was technical. Photocopy a poem, read it aloud, now write your own version on the same topic using this motif, or that technique. To be fair, I've seen the imitation exercise work, again and again, regardless of age or ability. Technically, par-ticipants are writing poems. But the win, for me, is empty.

I've done it myself. Sat paralyzed before the page, thinking, "This poem is neat and I am messy. This poem is practiced, published, 'right,' according to all of history and my workshop leader, which must make me 'wrong,' because I don't like it or I don't get it or I don't want to participate in this tradition at this time." Still, I did the work, searching for the literary technique in the model and then find-ing it in my own version. Never was I especially proud of this writing.

Where is joy? Where is play? Where is accident? Where is fail-ure? Where is risk and discovery? Isn't the tradition of imitation rooted in wonderment, in the love of another's words so profound that you must trace it to the letter? How do you inspire wonder-ment in your own workshop participants?

Maybe you ask them to do it–write, now, go!–without knowing how to. Hold off on the model text, strip away structure altogether,

and instead explore the creative impulse by hand, on
with Power, award-winning author and educator Pete1
a democratic teaching model founded in freewriting
increase in power and insight that comes from focusi
while at the same time putting aside your conscious con   ...g sen.
By releasing control over the way writing should sound, workshop
participants gain personal power, risking voice in their own wandering words. Maybe you study their writing for hints of energy, oddity, beauty, proof that writing is inherently imperfect—not practiced and published, trapped in some book, but an ongoing attempt, rife with revision. Maybe you introduce the model later, when participants' own words stake like flags on the page. "See here," you could point out, "this author does what you're doing, isn't that cool?"

Now that's writing with power.

Upon completion of the course, participants could very well:

» Engage in daily freewriting sessions

» Read their raw, unedited work aloud

» Draw from a living archive of multicultural texts as ready reference

» Honor their artistic mentors by researching a "family tree" of writers, musicians, filmmakers, etc., from whom their writing extends[11]

» Publish their work online and/or in a chapbook

» Perform their work at a public venue

Empower participants to do it "wrong" before they do it "right." Such an approach to the writing workshop teaches the twin goals of creativity and courage. Give them the gift of finding their own way in, both on the page through freewriting prompts, and off the page, by researching their individual artistic lineage. Trust that they can do it. And when they do, publish them, every single one, so that they, too, are experts.

4. Develop a critical vocabulary of craft

Workshop leaders like to claim that participants will develop a critical vocabulary of craft, though not literally—as in, develop the terminology together as a group so as to ensure egalitarian access to art-making. No. Instead, they insist participants should absorb the workshop leader's language and then imitate it. As is the trend with the traditional model, key information comes from the top down.

I'll never forget my first-ever writing workshop: the musty, makeshift library stocked with mismatched furniture and Bunsen-burnt coffee. Refusing to make eye contact, the other students shuffled the pages of my story back and forth. Finally, the professor broke the silence. "Felicia has a knack for rendering scene, don't you agree?" Rendering scene? I had no idea what he meant, but I'd earned my professor's approval, and that's all that mattered. Over time, I parroted phrases like "tonal shift" and "evocative voice" and "show, don't tell" back to my peers. Vocabulary served as status symbol: I was in the know.

If only I had spoken up, admitted to not knowing, then maybe I would've empowered others to do the same. It's as though tampering with art—dissecting it in pursuit of a mechanical heart—makes it somehow less pure. What's the old saying? You can't teach creative writing? Perhaps that's because craft itself is just another make-believe construction. Workshop leaders are equipped with approximate definitions, adapted to their individual aesthetic preferences. They guide by gut, intuiting when student writing "feels off," when it has "that certain wow quality."

Not only should workshop participants understand the craft of writing, but they should own the terms. In my classroom, we collectively define four target craft elements: voice, imagery, characterization, and arrangement (what participants insist on calling "flow"). We do this late into workshop, after much freewriting, so as not to inhibit the creative impulse. Participants really go in, grappling to make these abstract terms concrete. In the process, we talk about tiny, giant concepts, like when one participant asked, "What's an adjective, anyway? I've never understood that stuff." The fact that participants trust one another enough to confess what they don't understand about writing proves that we're working against a traditional workshop model that's rife with assumed knowledge. Instead, all students have equal access to the language of art, as defined by them. When we workshop, this shared vocabulary is on display so that we may speak about one another's work with deft precision.

In your own course, students could:

» Read a set of multicultural texts organized by craft element

» Discuss the texts in the context of craft

» Collectively define craft concepts

» Demonstrate use of craft concepts in short writing exercises

» Workshop using a shared vocabulary of target craft elements

» Reflect on the successes and challenges of craft in their own work

When workshop participants read for voice, for example, they're forced to ask, "Well, what is voice?" Likely they'll want the workshop leader to define the term for them so that they can engage in another search and find. Consider countering with, "What is voice, to you? And how does your definition influence the way you read and write?" When participants reconvene to compare definitions, they engage in collective meaning making. Moving forward, they're the experts, pointing to craft as a subjective authorial choice, not some immovable pillar of canonical white writing fundamentals. Participants are empowered to make informed aesthetic choices about their own work, and by extension, write from their own experiences. In doing so, they wrest craft from its white stronghold in homage to centuries of writers of color whose work proceeded the Western European tradition.

This philosophical quest is very Lynda Barry, whose graphic text *What It Is* defines craft (and creativity in general) as "the formless thing which gives things form."[12] She encourages us to track a wandering mind, to ask questions in answer to our questions, "to be able to stand not knowing long enough to let something alive take shape."[13] That "something alive" is the crux of craft.

5. Receive critique via workshop

Critique might very well be people of color's number one reason why not to join a writing workshop. To "receive critique" is to willingly assume a position of passivity: step away from the page, hands where I can see them, and don't talk back. Whether in pairs, small groups, or large group workshop, writers of color must sit silently and take it, "it" being the often tactless, likely long-winded, and predictably ignorant critique of their peers and workshop leader.

Lisa Lee, in her essay "Racial Invisibility and Erasure in the Workshop," provides a glimpse into the psychological ramifications of "taking it" upon submitting an excerpt of her novel to a graduate writing workshop:

> From the same novel, I submitted a different excerpt about a Korean American family experiencing racism in Napa, California. There was a scene where an adolescent brother and sister are practicing tennis with their mother at a country club. Four white middle-aged women are playing doubles on the adjacent court—two of them are blonde, tall, and thin, and one of them attacks the mother verbally with racist and misogynistic slurs. A tan, blonde bully, towering over the small Korean immigrant mother, both with rackets in hand. One of the men in the workshop—T, I will call him, white, I should mention—took issue with this. "This is such a stereotype!" T exclaimed. "This would never happen. It's totally unbelievable. This kind of racism would never happen to this family on a tennis court in Orange County. There are so many Asians in Orange County! This is such a stereotype!" T repeated. He went on: "I play tennis and there are all kinds of minorities playing tennis, not just white people, and nothing like that ever happens! Anyway, if somebody acts racist like this, then they're just low class." T was shouting and waving his arms.

The room was quiet. I was in shock. As the person being workshopped, you're not allowed to speak, but even if I had been, I was too shocked to have had a response.[14]

A white male peer calling into question the believability of Lee's narrative exposes a refusal on his part to engage with race. This scenario is unexceptional. And sometimes it is the professor who instigates refusal. Writers of color are charged with convincing white readers that our stories are believable, relatable, universal. Since there's no such thing as neutrality, what we're really charged with is erasing our bodies from our texts one by one until white readers feel dominant again, safe again. No wonder Lee expresses shock! Her sanity, positionality, and skill as writer are all under attack.

To the white egoist, workshop is prize arena for displays of control.

To writers of color, workshop is a potential trigger for shame, rage, anxiety, and/or depression.

The disparity is shocking, indeed. To get beyond workshop participants' passive receipt of critique and instead empower them to solicit targeted, craft-based feedback, ask yourself why you allow your students free rein to judge one another's work (first typed in letter format, as is the tradition, and then again, aloud in class). Is their critique a showcase of hard-earned editorial acumen, skills you've taught them alongside craft? No? Then level the playing field by training participants in the art of workshop. Without such training, workshop participants conflate kneejerk judgement with informed critique, exposing writers of color to lasting psychological and emotional damage.

Participants want to help one another. With proper training, workshop participants become capable of offering thoughtful, intelligent, and generous feedback on one another's writing. Rather than a competitive arena of ego and domination, workshop transforms into a human-to-human dialogue on authorial intent.

Over the course of the workshop, writers could participate in one or more of the following:

» Analyze critical essays and book reviews through a lens of race and feminist theories

>> Write a critical essay or book review on a work of their choosing

>> Train in Liz Lerman's Critical Response Process (see chapter 6)

>> Conduct a pre-workshop, one-on-one conference with the workshop leader

>> Moderate their own feedback sessions

>> Conduct a post-workshop, one-on-one conference with the workshop leader

Assuming I've trained my students well, a successful workshop means I'm the only one who is silent in the room. I challenge my-self to restrain the impulse to tell students how it's supposed to be done, and instead sit back and listen to their personal vision for the work. Isn't listening at the heart of critique? And yet we so often confuse it with the sound of our own voice.

6. *Demonstrate improvement in writing*

Often we task students with showcasing evidence of their learn-ing through a polished final draft. To pit first draft and final draft against one another is creative writing's version of a top-down sum-mative assessment: Have you changed what I told you to change in order to make your work better? Evidence of learning, then, is whether or not participants clued into the workshop leader's aes-thetic preferences. Morphing their writing to match earns high marks, whereas a refusal to listen results in low marks.

In graduate school, a white female professor once circled an entire page of my final essay and sighed. "I told you what to do here!" she said. "Why is it still the same?" Her exasperation was less invitation to dialogue about my personal preferences for the work, more scolding that I hadn't conformed to her opinion. Trusting my own artistic instincts meant she judged my process as a fail-ure. Had I "demonstrated improvement" by following orders, she might have regarded my work as a success.

To writers of color, this sort of exasperation is trite. We've got it. You want us to sound like you. Now what happens when we don't? When we won't?

A novice/master mentality sanctions summative assessment by positioning the workshop leader as supreme authority. Again and again, I see syllabi that charge participants with the responsibility of "improving their writing" with zero basis in what improvement looks like beyond that final, polished text. Is it technical (a post-workshop revision checklist)? Is it physical (an end-of-workshop reflective portfolio)? Is it psychological (a conquering of writing fears)? Is it emotional (a willingness to engage with complex material)? Is it civic (a thoughtful consideration of one's own work as well as the work of others)? As far as learning goes, a fixed final draft is awfully limiting.

By expanding our definition of "improvement" beyond a top-down model, we affirm that writing is a fluid, embodied process (see chapter 8). Let's relinquish control as workshop leaders and instead challenge participants to own their personal learning journeys. Imagine the possibilities!

Upon completion of this course, participants could:

» Acknowledge that writing is an inherently imperfect, ongoing process

» Debunk the myth of the muse by publicly articulating the hardships of writing, then brainstorming strategies for success

» Honor the creative process by summarizing the evolution of their work in formal artist statements

» Elicit targeted workshop feedback by posing specific, craft-based questions

» Assess the successes and challenges of each draft

» Revise a workshop draft (that first, experimental attempt) into a more fully realized first draft

» Craft a reflective portfolio that illustrates individual growth over time

» Celebrate the success of their artistic community by writing an end-of-workshop letter to their peers

Note that in the list above, the anti-racist version of improvement relies less on rubric, and more on participants' individual reflection on their ever-evolving technical, psychological, and emotional relationship to writing.

Too often participants abandon final drafts at the altar of the workshop leader's office, nervously awaiting a grade. What if, at the end of a writing workshop, participants knew exactly where they stood, because they managed their own progress from the get-go? What if, at the end of a writing workshop, participants didn't even care about a grade, because they stood firmly in their new power as writers? Allowing workshop participants to own their personal journeys advances a multidimensional definition of "improvement."

7. Study the rules of the English language

I do not teach grammar. Just the opposite, in fact. I encourage workshop participants to forgo grammatical rules in their freewriting exercises in order to stop thinking and start feeling—the way words stutter, swagger, sprint forward line by line in order to get at something urgent and infinitely more valuable than a rule, and that's raw energy. Creative writing is more about harnessing energy—the heart of an idea—than it is about imposing sterilized order, the "right" way to communicate. So when participants pointedly enroll in my workshop to improve their grammar, I tell them they're better off dropping.

This is not to say that grammar doesn't matter. Grammar matters, especially in courtrooms, police stations, schools, and hospitals. But I argue that its course of study belongs in a separate classroom, independent from the creative realm.

Speaking "properly" (commanding the rules of the English language) is a skill for which countless white strangers—baristas, cab drivers, teachers, neighbors, friends' parents—feel compelled to compliment me, proof that the brown-skinned person they envisage in their heads is Other. Then again, speaking "properly" (commanding the rules of the English language) is a skill for which countless people of color—family members, friends, strangers at bus stops and academic conferences—feel compelled to call me out on, proof that I *am* Other, trying to talk white. Many people of color "speak" in silence and sore feet, yelling-laughing and foiled-covered plates. There's code switching and language mixing. There's no one way, no one rule. How we speak is as abundant as we are.

In her essay "Crazy," Chris Stark shares how she had to "bend, twist, and break the rules of English to best get at different cultural experiences, realities, and awarenesses beyond 'white ways.'" She wrote a draft of her first novel, *Nickels*, while enrolled in a graduate MFA program, but chose not to workshop it in full because her professors and peers couldn't make sense of her Native protagonist's multiple, dissociative identities:

> I knew their reactions would stunt, disrupt, and perhaps stop my ability to get down the story. For example, parts of *Nickels* consist of a chorus of voices commenting on the protagonist's experiences. During workshop, a professor asked, "Is this like a Greek chorus?" Perhaps it is like a Greek chorus, but it is not a Greek chorus. It is something else that I don't necessarily know how to articulate. It does not have a name in English. Therefore, it does not exist in literature either. It is like music. It is like a pounding in the head. It is like a surge of energy. It is like all the hair on your head standing on end, connecting with the unseen.[15]

In choosing to forgo the parameters of grammatically correct English language—intentionally upsetting sentence structure, tense, point of view, and punctuation—Stark found freedom to write in a truer way, one that echoed Indigenous languages. I should note that when white writers attempt the same, forgoing story structure and grammatical rules in pursuit of complex meaning, they tend to win awards. Instead of eliciting confusion, hostility, and ridicule, as experienced by Stark and countless other people of color, white writers earn critical praise for their groundbreaking, genre-bending, meditative work.

I don't teach grammar because I want my workshop participants to experience freedom in their writing. If not in creative writing, where else can people of color pursue what Peter Elbow calls
"the wisdom of the tongue?"[16] Where else can they know best about
their own lives and consciousness, and not their white teachers,
peers, editors, historians, clergymen, scientists, politicians, journalists, and law enforcers?

Allowing your workshop participants to exercise voice in their
own voices sounds straightforward enough, and yet voice is creative
writing's most problematic paradox.

Put down the red pen. Resist writing over, crossing out, or correcting workshop participants' word choice. Instead, pursue the
impulse, the energy, the heart of an idea: "I don't understand this
yet, but I want to." In pursuit of that understanding, you might
independently expose yourself to a range of global writers and
their histories. In other words, what if you broadened your depth
of knowledge so that enactments of whiteness and its grammatical
tyranny no longer served as the standard for "good" writing?

What if, upon completion of the course, participants:

» Write daily in their own voices and read their work aloud

» Resist liking or not liking their drafts in an effort to achieve
   that essential, awake speech of their minds

» Pose questions about their writing in their own voices

» Write editorial notes on their own drafts during one-on-one
   conferences

» Study their writing to identify habits both conscious and
   unconscious

» Study multicultural storytelling tailored to their aesthetic

» Pursue an idea from workshop draft (that first, experimental
   attempt) into a more fully realized first draft

This type of writing hinges on discovery through the creative process itself; workshop participants do not set out to provide pre-determined answers that satisfy white bias, but instead pursue the raw, messy, spontaneous, personal questions that drive them. Participants proceed intuitively, transitioning in a way that may seem digressive but actually forms a clear path in retrospect. By reevaluating your priorities as workshop leader, you allow your participants to claim body, weight, and substance on the page.

Moving Forward with Real Membership

A twenty-first-century anti-racist writing workshop frees participants to exercise their own authentic voices. It expects participants to reflect on their own learning journeys. It trains participants in how to moderate their own workshop feedback. It ensures participants have equal access to the language of art, as defined by them. It empowers participants to do it "wrong" before they do it "right." It honors participants' influences, imaginations, and intellectual curiosities. And it affirms that every single one of them arrives at the classroom as experts in their own right, complete with a unique storytelling tradition.

This is the infrastructure that opens doors instead of closes them.

There's no moving forward without this infrastructure, even if your workshop remains predominantly white. As bell hooks reminds us, "It is so crucial that 'whiteness' be studied, understood, discussed—so that everyone learns that affirmation of multiculturalism, and an unbiased inclusive perspective, can and should be present whether or not people of color are present."[17] To choose not to use an infrastructure that centers multiculturalism is an active elimination of the lives of people of color from our collective consciousness.

If you really want to recruit writers of color, you've got to be about it, that much we've established. You must reevaluate your workshop's core principles as well as your own personal principles. That's tough work for all educators, regardless of our positionalities, so inundated are we in the long-standing principles of institutionalized white power. While the following example spotlights white allyship, critical self-examination is pertinent to everyone looking to decolonize their thinking to become more aware of what our students need across race and class.

Robin Diangelo, in her book *White Fragility: Why It's So Hard for White People to Talk about Racism*—a resource for white allies committed to anti-racism—spotlights the discomfort white people feel when discussing race, and how they ought to lean into that discomfort in order to build racial stamina:

> The key to moving forward is what we do with our discomfort. We can use it as a door out—blame the messenger and disregard the message. Or we can use it as a door in by asking, Why does this unsettle me? What would it mean for me if this were true? How does this lens change my understanding of racial dynamics? How can my unease help reveal the unexamined assumptions I have been making? Is it possible that because I am white, there are some racial dynamics that I can't see? Am I willing to consider that possibility? If I am not willing to do so, then why not?[18]

Maybe, while reading this chapter, you've felt attacked, shamed, or judged. Maybe you've felt defensive, argumentative, or in need of absolution, because none of this applies to you, you get it, you're down. If so, I suggest meditating on Diangelo's questions above.

To transform the creative classroom paradigm, we must sustain discomfort, listen deeply, and reflect on the unsettling truth that white racism is inevitable. Only then can we endeavor change.

A twenty-first-century anti-racist writing workshop leader concedes that neutrality, objectivity, universality, and normality do not exist. The workshop leader relinquishes an egoistic interest in domination, control, and manipulation. The workshop leader engages in listening over speaking, in process over product. And the workshop leader broadens their knowledge of global authors and their histories in order to actively counter an aesthetic based on white writers. "Tell me what to read," allies often ask, and though this book and other online literary arts resources like De-Canon: A Visibility Project put forth introductory appendixes of contemporary US writers of color, the impetus must ultimately come from you, the anti-racist reader-thinker-teacher, from the fruits of your own learning journey.[19]

Recruiting writers of color means reflecting on your biases and airing out your teaching habits, reading and re-reading outside of your comfort zone, and then preparing a living archive of scanned print material, sourced pdfs, and multimedia art to serve as ready resource. Then, and only then, are you ready to go about recruitment. It's time—it's long been time—to offer writers of color a place to belong, on purpose.

A Preliminary Survey

Imagine if your writers of color self-advocated for success in your workshop. Likely they'd survey your syllabi—what you teach—but imagine if they went a step further, inquiring about *how* you teach? Are you prepared with answers?

Kathy Luckett and Shannon Morreira at the University of Cape Town's Humanities Education Development Unit argue that beyond the content of what you teach, it's just as important to change assumptions in your "hidden curriculum," those personal principles so embedded in how you teach that you probably take them for granted.[20]

As a starting point, reflect on the following survey, adapted from a working group discussion led by Luckett and Morreira in 2017. Freewrite your responses with the goal of total transparency, the most effective starting point for assessment.

» For whom do you design your curriculum? In other words, who is your ideal, imagined student? What assumptions do you make about their background?

» What norms and values inform your curriculum choices?

» Do you articulate your own positionality when lecturing? Why or why not?

» Does your curriculum reflect its geographic location, including subjugated histories, cultures, and languages?

» How does your teaching legitimate the experiences and cultures of students of color?

» How does your teaching affirm the agency of students of color?

» How does your curriculum require white students to acquire the intellectual and cultural resources to function effectively in a plural society?

» How do you build a community in your classroom where students learn actively from each other and draw on their own knowledge sources?

» What can you do to make your assessment criteria show what all students are capable of, drawing on their strengths and promoting their agency and creativity?

» Now ask yourself, am I ready to prepare my headspace for change?

CHAPTER TWO

Fostering Engagement, Mindfulness, and Generosity

Mothering Our Writers

I'm in an interdepartmental committee meeting that's run long, well past the time I told my husband I'd be home to relieve him as caretaker for our son. I imagine him watching the driveway for my car, bored of the banality, preoccupied with his own work obligations, angry, maybe, that I didn't just walk out of my meeting when I realized the time. More likely the anger's imposed, a fossil lodged in my chest from my own years pacing the window: watching, waiting, frantic for the sound of the garage door, the car door, my husband's muffled voice on the cell phone.

Outside sounds.

Inside, I was learning how to mother, a marathon of self-suppression, discipline, and labor. Order and obedience, call and response, an everyday endurance fraught with claustrophobia. Inside, I was learning how to listen, a full body meditation like some sort of postpartum superpower: The stirrings, the coughs, the pitch shift in cry. The threat of a doorbell during nap. The clatter of keys that meant my husband was home and I could finally shower, pretend to

47

be one person again instead of this newfound trinity: baby, mother, and me.

I choose to stay in the committee meeting because we're talking about how to best serve our senior thesis writing students. "It's not like we prepare them at all," a white female colleague sighs. "And suddenly they've got these high-stakes, long-term writing projects with zero skills to cope."

It's true, I think. Writing is hard, physically, mentally, and emotionally. When working one-on-one with senior thesis students a couple of years back, I remember how dependent they were on their advisors for affirmation. If the advisor was happy with the thesis, the student was happy; if the advisor was unhappy (dissatisfied, perhaps, or inattentive, slow to respond or vague in their feedback) the student was doomed to despair, the crippling kind that resulted in weeks of no work. Rather than elicit ownership and resourcefulness, the thesis spiked students' anxiety; they wanted their advisors to tell them exactly how to do it "right."

"I found it helpful to listen to them," I say. "I used to meet with a group of thesis students every week to check in about their states of mind. They'd talk about what they were proud of, or afraid of, or nervous about when it came to writing. A lot of the time the students expressed feeling isolated, like they were the only ones who were falling behind or were sick of their topic. Listening to one another took the pressure off the thesis as product and helped switch their thinking to the writing process. The questions became: How can I best manage my stress, because isn't self-care just as important as the writing?"

At this a white male colleague scoffs. "I mean, doesn't that detract from the whole purpose of the thesis? We want students to struggle on their own. Without struggle, what do they learn? It's not our job to mother them."

"True," my female colleague consents, and they continue to troubleshoot for another fifteen minutes or so. But I'm stuck on his use of "mother," how easily it slipped from his mouth, and with such ready reception: Oh no, we don't want that, you're absolutely right. Because mother equals woman, and woman equals feminine, soft, powerless.

To listen to our students—to allow them voice—is to somehow give in to them, ruin them, a mother coddling her spoiled children.

But that can't be right, I think. Mothering, for me, means will-power, fortitude, grit. It is the transcendent power to multiply oneself, succeeded by the supreme humility to serve that second self. Listening is an extension of that humility, a tribute to the fact that none of us are alone. We are multitudes, mothered again and again in rhythm with time.

As a professor of color, I'd "mothered" my writers since jump, taking on the extra, invisible labor of serving as mentor, inspiration, guide, and confidant to my workshop participants of color, while simultaneously attending to my white students' volatile grappling with race and racism, often for the first time in their lives. A good deal of my day was dedicated to listening.

Why must listening and learning be posed as antithetical when we know they are symbiotic?

Why does emotional care undermine intellectual growth in my colleagues' minds?

And why are white faculty seemingly exempt from this emotional labor?

Because I cannot articulate these questions on cue, I stay silent; the meeting adjourns, and I reclaim my post at home. Still, "mother" troubles me.

The problem is perspective. In order for my colleagues to understand my viewpoint, they would have to step from product to process.

A product-based mentality supports academic experts as independent egos, gendered masculine, hard, and powerful. They do the talking, and students do the listening. They want students to struggle on their own, at which point they tear the work down to make it stronger, driving students toward the "right" way, the "true" knowledge.

This is what Brazilian educator and philosopher Paulo Freire calls the "banking system of education," in which "students are the depositories and the teacher is the depositor." Rather than engage in real dialogue with students—an act of love and humility that subverts

the teacher's authority and elevates students to critical co-investiga-
tors—the teacher's task is to talk at students, "issu[ing] communiques
and mak[ing] deposits which the students patiently receive, memorize, and repeat."[1] The ultimate goal of the banking system is to
groom students' passivity so as to better indoctrinate them into the
dominant (white) culture. "Translated into practice," Freire writes,
"this concept is well suited to the purposes of the oppressors, whose
tranquility rests on how well people fit the world the oppressors have
created, and how little they question it."[2] Shut down dialogue, and
you shut down authentic thinking, liberation, and freedom.

The banking model best serves privileged white males, whose
easy access to voice is secure, whose legacy of supremacy is safe.
They see themselves mirrored in their college professors: auton-
omous, authoritative, revered. To "struggle on their own" means
drawing on their extensive systemic resources. Institutionalized
power positions them well to compete in the classroom. They're
better prepared to prove themselves on the page because they're
not overstretched proving themselves damn near everywhere else. A
banking system of education inherently disservices students of col-
or, whose centralized racial identity—a direct influence on voice—is
denied as credible currency. It underserves students of color who
do not seem themselves mirrored in positions of power in the academy. To "struggle on their own" is yet another attempt at erasure.

"College is hard," a family friend commented at dinner the
other night. He was trying to convince his sixteen-year-old daughter,
an aspiring writer, to attend a historically Black college, just as he
and his wife did decades previous. "You've got these Black kids,
top of their class, best at everything in high school. Then they hit
college, and, all of a sudden, they're just mediocre. It really messes
with them."

It was difficult for me not to jump in here, to vocalize my discomfort: "Mediocre compared to whom, white people?!" The fallacy
that no matter how prepared people of color are academically, they
will fall short when measured against their white peers, really gets at
me. But I stopped myself from reacting, and chose to listen instead.

What he was getting at, I gathered, was confidence, not assessment; people, not papers. His daughter understood instinctively.

"But I feel like I have a really good sense of myself," she replied. "I've got a strong base."

"Good," her dad said, shaking his head. "Because college is hard."

Here "hard" means something different from the gendered, masculine, product-based mentality favored by my colleagues. This family friend, this dad, was trying to mother his daughter by dialoguing with her about the very real psychological challenges a person of color faces in college.

You better trust, eighteen-year-old me believed that I, too, had a good sense of myself; that I, too, had a strong base. In retrospect, I was severely unprepared for the psychic weight of race during my first year at Wellesley College. I thought being good at school was fuel enough to carry me the two thousand miles from Albuquerque, New Mexico, to Wellesley's Munger Hall. Once on campus, I distorted into a funhouse mirror reflection: poorer and browner and shorter than ever before. The shock of it—East Coast wealth— messed with me, indeed. Rather than merely demonstrate *learning* in class, I sought to prove my *worth*: my exhausting "I-belong-here!" performance wrung me of joy. I got all A's that first semester. Of course I did; the stakes had never been higher. And yet my sense of inferiority festered. I couldn't shake my warped reflection.

"You're such an anomaly," a white female professor mused, handing back my A+ paper. Hearing the words aloud felt violent.

Because the majority of post-secondary institutions are microcosms of white supremacy, people of color endure relentless affronts to our racial identities from the classroom to the dorm room and everywhere in between. There are ominously few opportunities for relief. Mentorship is scarce because so few of our professors look like us; those who do are often burned out from the exhausting emotional labor of being the on-call POC representative. Compound that by the stressors we internalize (feeling angry, unsupported, alienated, misunderstood, unsafe, devalued, exoticized, and/or invisible), people of color must draw on profound inner strength to cope. Instinct tells us to bolt, go back, give up. Practicing self-care is key to our college success.

This is the first challenge of diversifying your writing workshop: retaining your students of color. In the anti-racist model, white faculty share the burden of intentional cultural self-education so as to actively support every student. Were you to check in with participants about how they're doing, what they're thinking, prompting them to vocalize their insights and fears, your classroom might very well serve as one of those rare opportunities for relief, a space in which to feel like a full person again.

"Mothering" our students by listening—allowing space for them to use their voices—is an act of humility, it's an act of conspiring toward mutual learning. When I first had my son, I thought there's no way it's possible, passing down this burden of how to be a person: a good boy, a just man. The responsibility felt overwhelming. It wasn't until later, when I realized just how much I had changed since giving birth, that it dawned on me: My son is training me in how to be a person, too. Teaching is reciprocal.

It's what Paulo Freire calls a "humanist" approach to education, a methodology "imbued with a profound trust in people and their creative power."[3] Teacher and student are partners, jointly responsible for knowledge construction. For Freire cautions, "Without dialogue there is no communication, and without communication there can be no true education."[4] Students deserve your commitment to their agency. Let's model healthy and sustainable learning rooted in communication.

This chapter trains workshop leaders in how to mother their writers, a practice that honors process: Who writes, and why, and where, and when, and how? This, so different from what we write, but nonetheless important. Passivity is not an option. Writers must actively address the physical, mental, emotional, and cultural barriers that prevent their full creative realization. They must name their fears and write anyway. No longer objectified as papers, workshop participants evolve in professors' eyes as multidimensional people, sharing together in a workshop that values engagement, mindfulness, and generosity.

Engagement

I recently asked a white female friend what her anti-racist workshop approach looked like in action, and she fumbled. "Yeah. Hmmm. I don't know. I guess I'm a softie. I'm really flexible about deadlines. I mean, the students get me the work eventually." I single her out not because her response is problematic, necessarily, but because it's illustrative of a liberal white interpretation of anti-racism: that people of color (typecast as "inner-city kids" to disguise racial animus) are "diverse," and therefore require policies that accommodate our "special" circumstances (insert scene from any movie featuring young people of color, ever).

As a feminist scholar, I used to think that this sort of adaptive teaching policy was fair, in that it respected the burdensome work/life/school/family balance that I myself managed as an undergraduate. It wasn't until I began teaching in Chicago public high schools that I learned that deadlines were irrelevant. If a student was truly engaged, they would find the time to write, be it on the subway, during downtime at work, during math class, whatever. The words would materialize, and so would they, again and again. But only if they cared.

How do you make them care? Start by making them accountable.

Strategy one: attendance accountability

Your workshop participants of color don't need you to soften your policies for them. Just the opposite. Try demanding more of them: Show up, on time, every time. Well-meaning colleagues have criticized my mandatory attendance policy as unnecessarily harsh and unrealistic. But a lesson I want to impress upon my workshop participants is that life is a series of conspiracies to keep us from exercising voice. To be a writer is to choose to write, to show up every day and do the work. There's always an excuse not to. My attendance policy posits that choice:

> » Miss one day of class, and your final grade will decrease by one half letter grade.

» Arrive late to class four times, and your final grade will decrease by one half letter grade.

» Miss workshop, and you risk failure.

Read "final grade" as "commitment to your creative power." Because it takes commitment—not borne out of fear, but out of accountability—I owe it to myself and the workshop to choose writing—in order to truly care.

I e-mail this attendance policy to every participant well in advance of the first day of workshop, only to receive polite requests that I pardon students' "special" circumstances. At the predominantly white liberal arts college where I work, this means an athlete's away games, a family vacation abroad, a great aunt's birthday celebration, a camping trip, a concert. Sometimes it's acute anxiety or depression. I make it clear to these students that my attendance policy is firm. As artists we evolve season by season, some of which are more conducive to a daily writing commitment than others. If it's not time, don't force it, I tell them, because forcing it is missing it. Some of my most successful writers use workshop to process their emotional hardship, but they are unequivocal about showing up and putting in the work. It is up to the student to choose.

Workshop leaders might fear that a firm stance on attendance and deadlines will dissuade writers of color from enrolling, but I've observed, again and again, that my participants respect the demand for accountability, as it implies that I will take them, and their work, seriously.

The first lesson of workshop, then, is participants' honest self-analysis: Are they prepared to embrace accountability and commit to a writing collective?

Strategy two: foster community

"I enter the classroom with the assumption that we must build community in order to create a climate of openness and intellectual rigor," bell hooks explains in *Teaching to Transgress*. "I think that a feeling of community creates a sense that there is shared commitment and a common good that binds us." That common good is participants' creative power. With time, you can feel it: every single person is present in their power. To get there, workshop participants must concede that their individual voices matter. "It has been my experience that one way to build community in the classroom is to recognize the value of each individual voice . . . To hear each other (the sound of different voices), to listen to one another, is an exercise in recognition. It also ensures that no student remains invisible in the classroom."[5] The anti-racist writing workshop is a pedagogy of deep listening—to oneself, to one's workshop leader, and to every member of the collective—ensuring equal access to voice. This is the sort of communication that makes for a successful arts community.

If you visit my classroom, you'll hear music, low, playing in the background—my song selections at first, until I invite participants to bring in their own music to share. Workshop hasn't yet begun, but most students are present, seated at tables arranged into a circle. They're sharing food that a classmate brought in, a snack policy that I institute on the first day of workshop; everyone signs up for one day. I launched this policy ten or so years ago on the grounds that my workshop participants were often hungry and therefore unable to exercise the mental and emotional endurance workshop requires. Back then it was me who provided snack, sensitive not to overburden my low-income students' budgets. That is, until those students asked if they could cover a day. There's an uncomplicated joy to food—whether it be homemade bread or a piece of fruit—that feels a lot like creativity. It's a gift, and participants are proud to share with one another.

We begin class by thanking our snack host by name, followed by a round of applause. Next, we commence check-in, a daily ritual in which I address workshop participants one at a time, by name, asking, "How are you doing?" This, my method of roll call, elicits a lot of embarrassed shrugs on day one. It kills participants to be so visible; they're "cool," they're "fine," they've got nothing else to add. Steadily, over time, they elaborate, and we hear about a break-in, a breakup, an illness, a friend who's in town, a new job. Sometimes participants use check-in to troubleshoot with the group about their writing. Sometimes they use it to communicate with me that they're in a bad place that day, period. That's my official spiel on check-in: it helps me to gauge where each student is that day so that I may tailor my teaching to best respond to them.

Unofficially, check-in is about community.

We learn each other's names, without even meaning to.

We embrace vulnerability by sharing our individual experiences.

We listen to one another, recognize one another, root for one another.

We evolve into a collective, an arts community to which we feel responsible. It matters if we are not present.

The key to check-in is that the workshop leader participates, too. Once, a student e-mailed me a note of encouragement when I, bleary eyed, informed the class that today was an "ostrich day." My toddler was sick for the third time that month and all I wanted to do was bury my head in the sand, preferably forever. "You're a role model to us girls," she wrote. "You keep it real. You don't hide the fact that you have a lot to balance, but trust that you do everything really, really well." I've used check-in to discuss fears about my writing, about motherhood, about our country and my place in it, alongside frivolous anecdotes, like the time I loaded a shopping cart's worth of groceries into a stranger's unlocked car. Communication, and by extension, community, renders us all human. It's this human-to-human connection that enables us to see, hear, and support one another in an anti-racist workshop model.

Strategy three: make writing relevant

The third and final strategy for engaging students is to make writing relevant. This means building on accountability and vulnerability in order to engender trust.

I top load my workshops with highly personal writing exercises, beginning with a first day freewrite: Declare why you are good at writing. Participants must own the language, meaning they can't parrot another's words (My third-grade teacher once said . . .). After they've generated a short list, I ask that they choose one, stand up, and say it aloud (My name is . . ., and I'm good at writing because . . .). At this point, we cheer annoyingly loud so as to disrupt every other class in the building. My students' voices shake when they share, because it's scary to stake a claim: I am worthy of words on the page. The physical act of standing, understandably enough, is most contentious here.[6] Participants will beg to shrink themselves. Don't let them.

The more direct and ambitious those initial freewriting exercises, the better. This means prompting participants to write about themselves—why they write—their motivation, their unspoken desires—and then push them to share that writing out loud, daily, with the workshop. These early, intimate confessionals command trust. They also set high stakes for what's to come: when participants later attempt a poem, or a play, or an essay, it's imbued with significance beyond the task itself. That poem, that play, that essay is a triumph over all of the reasons not to write. How trivial showmanship and competition become when you make writing personal to the author.

Gloria Anzaldúa, in "Speaking in Tongues: A Letter to Third World Women Writers," speaks of the psychological and cultural barriers that prevent so many writers of color from putting words on the page:

> The voice recurs in me: Who am I, a poor Chicanita from the sticks, to think I could write? How dare I even consider becoming a writer as I stooped over the tomato fields bending, bending under the hot sun, hands broadened and calloused, not fit to hold the quill, numbed into an animal stupor by the heat . . . How hard it is for us to think we can choose to become writers, much less feel and believe that we can. What have we to contribute, to give? Our own expectations condition us. Does not our class, our culture as well as the white man tell us writing is not for women such as us?[7]

That voice is in all of us, sneering ridicule that ricochets in the mind every time we attempt to liberate ourselves. And yet Anzaldúa pushes beyond the barriers, urging herself and others to write:

> I write to record what others erase when I speak, to rewrite the stories others have miswritten about me, about you. To become

more intimate with myself and you. To discover myself, to preserve myself, to make myself, to achieve self-autonomy . . . To convince myself that I am worthy and that what I have to say is not a pile of shit. To show that I can and that I will write, never mind their admonitions to the contrary. And I will write about the unmentionables, never mind the outraged gasp of the censor and the audience. Finally, I write because I'm scared of writing but I'm more scared of not writing.[8]

How rare, the opportunity to hear from writers of color about why they write, despite a lifetime's insistence to the contrary. It makes art take on a higher purpose. The collective stands in witness to this transformation.

As a former student states in her end-of-term course evaluation:

I felt I had no choice but to give it my all because I would not only be cheating the class, but myself. It was not a superficial class. It got to the dirt of who we are, why we must write. Felicia did an amazing job of allowing us to be open because then we could see our fears and inhibitions reflected in the words of other people. After that, it was obvious I had to write and be honest.

To engage your workshop participants, you must make them accountable to their purpose as writers. A writer listens. A writer is vulnerable. A writer trusts that they are worthy of words on the page, despite the voices that say otherwise. This is creative power. Help them claim it.

Mindfulness

Mindfulness is an energy of awareness, meaning that you are both physically and psychologically planted in the present moment. When you write, you write with your whole body, not rushing or multitasking or compartmentalizing the assignment but rather relinquishing control, surrendering to the creative impulse. When you read, you read with perspective and open intention, harnessing a wandering mind. When you listen, you receive another's words without judgement or defensiveness, that egoistic impulse that mistakes the sound of your own voice with being smart or right. And when you rest, you aim for outward and inward attunement so that you may return to the work revitalized.

Mindfulness is openness, a certain state of mind that comes about when we get out of the damn way.

This might sound a bit ambitious for a workshop. But writing is so much more than a technical skillset, marks on a page made right or wrong. That's product. We're people, and as such, we need to address writing as process, a psychological habit that we've cultivated for years without much, if any, consideration.

"In daily life we're disconnected from ourselves," teaches Thích Nhất Hạnh in *The Art of Communicating*. "We're alive, but we don't know that we're alive. Throughout the day, we lose ourselves. To stop and communicate with yourself is a revolutionary act."[9] In learning to listen to ourselves, we're more fully aware of our creative energy, better able to understand and listen to others.

Reflection

To begin, I ask that my workshop participants reflect on when, where, and how they write. The similarities are startling: late at night, in their rooms, by computer, prone to interruption by roommates or family members, a vibrating cell phone, a chiming inbox, a cache of social media on the screen. The goal is to get the work done and then move on to the next thing. When I ask participants to bring in three samples of their past writing in order to examine paragraph length, sentence structure, and word choice, it becomes very clear very fast that in getting the work done, they unconsciously employ a set of go-to strategies: writing habits. This is true even of participants who agonize, word by word, over their text, who do not rush but rather suffer through the task. With time, participants start to conflate their writing habits with their identity as writers; their voice, their style. Challenge the habit and you condemn the writer. This is the very opposite of mindfulness. Closed off to their own creative potential, participants are stuck on autopilot.

To kick off my workshop, then, I inform participants that a goal of the class is to nurture mindfulness. To be physically present is one thing, but to be wholly present, to tune into their work, themselves, and the writing collective, is another.

Writing by hand

As a daily practice, students power down and stow their cell phones and laptops in favor of writing by pen, on paper (with accommodations to allow for alternative methods). This does not go over well, predictably so. Because really, who wants to change? Our habits are comfortable to us. Still, participants persist in writing by hand in an effort to purge the conduit—the keyboard, the screen—and tap directly into the energy of their moving minds.

In *Syllabus*, Lynda Barry reflects on the power of hand to page:

> I began keeping a notebook in a serious way when I met my teacher Marilyn Frasca in 1975 at The Evergreen State College in Olympia, Washington. She showed me ways of using these simple things—our hands, a pen, and some paper—as both a navigation and expedition device, one that could carry me into my past, deeper into my present, or farther into a place I have called "the image world"—a place we all know, even if we don't notice this knowing until someone reminds us of its ever-present existence . . . This practice can result in what I've come to consider a wonderful side effect: a visual or written image we call "a work of art," although a work of art is not what I'm after when I'm practicing this activity. What am I after? I'm after what Marilyn Frasca called "being present and seeing what's there."[10]

Instead of training your workshop participants in how to get the work done, why not train them in how to slow down and see what's there? The notebook is an entry point, the writing a journey, a process of discovery that reveals itself over time. The goal is to be present, patient, to both give and receive the words.

Writing by hand certainly takes the pressure off getting it "right," the perfectionism that petrifies so many talented writers. Our bright white screens make it neat and easy to erase any evidence of an attempt. The physical, forward momentum of the pen compels us to write now and edit later. And so, to the great relief of workshop participants' overburdened brains, they exercise mindfulness by separating the writing task into stages: create in the moment, edit later, revise last. I talk more specifically about daily writing rituals in chapter 3, but the point is that putting hand to page jolts students out of autopilot, opening up new possibilities in their writing.

An added bonus, writing can now take place anywhere, unplugged. We revisit our survey of when, where, and how participants write, and then pointedly mix it up: write in the early morning, with music; write in the afternoon, outside, somewhere green; write at night, in a diner; integrate a walk into the middle of your writing session. Sometimes it's as simple as turning off their cell phones. Participants often discover a surprising consequence of a change in routine: the words come easier.

Tuning inward—the revolutionary act of defying autopilot to more deeply communicate with ourselves—achieves a certain mindset, described here by a former student:

> I remember hearing that the objective was not a product, but a "state of mind." I found this to be true, yet I wasn't sure just what it meant at the start. In many academic classes, doing the bare minimum, or only what is required of you, is enough to get a good grade and to learn something. This class is different. It stayed with me all the time—on walks, before going to sleep, in showers, in conversations with friends, etc. I didn't even need to put in effort to be working, which just goes to show how relevant and personal this course was to me, and to all of us.

Mindfulness does more than push students to break with old writing habits and unlock their creative power. It also helps achieve an anti-racist workshop agenda. White institutional customs of control and domination are ingrained in participants' psyches. To disrupt these habits, workshop participants must engage in ongoing self-awareness. The goal is twofold: students' mindfulness of their nonverbal and verbal communication.

Any workshop leader knows the power of body language. Students slumped at their desks is the obvious example, but there's also that jiggling knee, those tapping fingers, the sigh, the eye roll, the refusal to make eye contact, all nonverbal tactics of silencing one another. Tuning students in to how their bodies speak helps ease workshop relations—we are all responsible for checking ourselves so that our egos do not overtake the room. In the midst of workshop, I pause to remind students to tune into their bodies. We'll take a breath, sit upright, and continue. "Why don't you take a moment?" I'll prompt individual participants, should their nonverbal contributions become oppressively loud. A trip to the bathroom, a sip of water, and then they're present again, more fully engaged in the art of listening.

Of course it comes down to listening. Humility, at the heart of connection.

Talking, too, is a lesson in listening. Thích Nhất Hạnh calls mindful speech "Right Speech," a conscious choice to replace violent words—"speech that lacks openness"—with words of compassion and tolerance.[11] The goal of Right Speech is to truly hear and understand the other person, not to judge them against ourselves. For the purposes of workshop, this means asking questions of the artist so that we may better understand their goals for the work (something I discuss in depth in chapter 6). Ego urges us to manipulate others' writing so that it more closely adheres to our own aesthetic preferences—Let me tell you how to make it better—an act of aggression against writers of color who seek to claim their own voice on the page. Mindfulness necessitates an inversion of power: "Why don't you tell me what you want to achieve, and together we can work toward your goal?" Over time, workshop participants succeed in nurturing openness and awareness in themselves and their writing. Creativity becomes an emergent process rather than a static skill, evidenced here in another end-of-term reflection: "After this course, I am looking at everything differently; I'm examining the world in a new light. It's like I'm looking at the world through a pair of lenses that are a Venn diagram of logic, creativity, and potentiality. It's incredible."

Generosity

Generosity is a study in who writes, a concept which startles my workshop participants: Who else would it be, if not me?

Well, fear, of course.

Facebook fed me a meme recently, something along the lines of, "Do what you love, and you'll never work another day in your life (unless you become a writer, in which case you'll toil tirelessly and suffer a lifetime of self-doubt)." As a culture, we normalize a writer's neuroses; anxiety, insecurity, doubt, indecision, and procrastination are synonymous with art-making. To write is to embody negativity. We unconsciously surrender our creativity to fear.

A product-based mentality only exacerbates this suffering, due to its emphasis on a polished final outcome. With that mentality, a blank page conjures fear of failure and rejection; a first draft is imperfect and therefore bad; a final draft is poorly reviewed by a professor or agent and therefore of no value. Fear wants to exercise control, strangling the life energy from our words until they are flawless. But real writing, the pursuit of authentic voice through process, not product, is a release of control.

Your workshop participants can reclaim their creativity, release control, and restore confidence in their work by exercising generosity toward themselves.

Facing Fear

In *Writing Past Dark: Envy, Fear, Distraction, and Other Dilemmas in the Writer's Life*, Bonnie Friedman states, "Talent is not rare. What's rare is the devotion and stamina to keep writing. . . . Caring for the writerly self is a decisive component in being able to keep writing, and writing better. For there is only one essential correlation when it comes to writing, and that's simply between those who write and those who become writers."[12] Caring for the writerly self, while gendered feminine (as opposed to the masculine, manic-depressive's bravado and alcoholism) is essential to participants' long-term success, yet rarely is it addressed as a workshop skill.

To rally a new generation of multicultural writers, you must start at the heart: participants' emotional relationship to writing. The anti-racist writing workshop trains participants in how to release fear's stranglehold over their work and exercise authentic voice.

At the top of class, I address participants' fear of risk-taking, for if there are no words, there is no workshop. The blank page cannot win, and so I ask: "What are your excuses for staying immobilized?" Sometimes it's fear of imperfection. Sometimes it's fear of sounding stupid, or doing it wrong, or airing out stories better kept private. "Write a list of your writing fears," I instruct my students. "Don't hold anything back." After they freewrite for ten minutes or so, I draw on an exercise from *Writing Past Dark*. "Review your list," I instruct, "and organize your fears into two categories." The first is internal (I'm afraid of betraying my dad if I share this), and the second is external (I'm afraid the class won't understand my writing). It's a rare workshop participant with balanced columns; usually the consensus is one of shock: "I'm the one keeping me from writing!" Or, "I never realized I cared so much what other people think!"

After some discussion, participants once more return to their list. Next to each fear, they add, "But I will write anyway." We stand and share these fears aloud, as many rounds as workshop participants are willing, followed by the mantra, "But I will write anyway." Not only does this exercise prompt participants to deconstruct patterns of writer's block, procrastination, and playing it safe (patterns previously normalized as par for the creative course), it also confirms that they are not alone in their fear. We channel poet Tanaya Winder's acronym: Fiercely Embrace Ancestral Resilience: "I want to reframe fear so that it doesn't own me. Rather, I want to remember my mother, my grandmother, and all my ancestors whenever I am afraid. I want their strength and ancestral resilience to ground me."[13]

Removing Competition

As workshop progresses and participants share their writing aloud daily, we address the impulse to compete. Our compulsion to compare ourselves to the group is as spontaneous as breathing, another unexamined norm of creative writing culture. And so we put in the work. I ask participants to reflect on that moment when art-making became less joy and more suffering: How do I measure up? Am I any good, compared to him, compared to her? Or am I just wasting my time? They freewrite scenes from their past that tainted writing from imaginative play into a criterion of self-worth. When did competition kick in, and how has it affected your work? The point is to remind participants that art-making is innate to all of us. It's when our adult brains interfere that we compromise our confidence.

I go on to ask how competition affects our art collective. When someone reads in workshop, are participants genuinely receptive to their work? Or are they trapped in dualistic judgement: "He is good and I am bad." Writers rarely speak on it, but duality is toxic. At best, it transforms others' successes into a personal affront to our own talent (Why did she get published, when I'm better than her?). At worst, it keeps us paralyzed, because "Why even bother to write if I'll never be as good as so and so?" Instead, we aim for equilibrium: "He is good and I am good." "We are not the same writer, necessarily so, but I can learn from him." Confronting the impulse to compete head-on is healthy for workshop participants, as they air out the negativity that stifles so many writing communities.

As we go on to prepare drafts, we tackle our tendency to embody criticism. When I introduce myself as a writer at gatherings, strangers will often confide how they could never put themselves out there like that. "The criticism!" What they don't realize is that a writer is their worst critic. This internal critic, it takes hold of the best of us. To ignore it is ineffective and results in a heap of stressful and debilitating psychic correspondence. Instead, I encourage my workshop participants to create distance between themselves and their critical thoughts by physically writing out the words their internal critic says.

When we're immersed in a substantial writing task, I'll ask participants to take a moment and freewrite: "What does your internal critic say about you today? What does it say about your writing?" Participants release these thoughts onto the page, witness the words in print, and then ignore them, acknowledging that the critic is just fear speaking. Because no matter how well I train my workshop participants in giving and receiving feedback, if they only believe their internal critic, they'll never grow as writers. They must compartmentalize the fear and move on.

Finally, in preparation for workshop and one-on-one conferences, I caution my students not to confuse their writing with the need for approval. We dedicate a freewrite session to untangling participants' projects from their emotional needs. "What specific feedback do you need on your draft in order to better achieve your writing goals?" I begin, followed by, "Now ask yourself, what do I need right now, on an emotional level?"

Maybe the student is spent from excavating difficult memories; the writing is raw and in need of organization. So why, then, does she cry when provided with guidance? Maybe she's conflated herself with her work, a common practice among writers. What she needs is rest and confirmation that her courage paid off by seeking out a trusted friend to champion her draft in advance of workshop. Had she confronted her emotional needs early on, she could have exercised the necessary self-care. Thus refreshed, she'd be better able to receive the workshop's feedback, not confusing it with commentary on herself.

Try as we might, no writing collective or workshop leader can fulfill a writer's emotional needs. But with practice, participants can learn to exercise generosity toward themselves, a skill worth cultivating for a long-term writing career. Even better, then, when the workshop leader goes on to afford openhanded praise.

A former student reflects:

> Felicia supported students in not just class decisions but in life decisions. Not only did the course allow me to intentionally carve out time to commit fully to my writing, I learned a lot about my own writing process. I figured out how to cope with slow work days as well as get the most out of my most productive days. More than anything, it allowed me to connect with other students sharing in the same sorts of ups and downs. We each got the chance

to share about our work and rejuvenate our energy, passion, and focus towards our writing.

This is what generosity toward oneself, and one another, does when it is put into action.

Mothering Myself

I'm afraid that no one will read this book.

I'm afraid that I'll lose friends over this book.

I'm afraid that white readers will threaten or verbally assault me for writing this book.

I'm afraid that POC readers won't take my ideas seriously because I'm not Chicana enough.

I'm afraid that educators won't take my ideas seriously because I'm too young, or at least I look too young.

I'm afraid that white selection committees won't hire me as a result of writing this book.

I'm afraid that people from my past will accuse me of lying.

I'm afraid that people from my past will hurt because of what I've written.

I'm afraid that the responsibilities of motherhood will keep me from finishing this book.

I'm afraid that I won't be able to afford a book tour.

I'm afraid that this book will not be good enough.

I'm afraid that no one will care and nothing will change.

But I will write anyway.

CHAPTER THREE

Instituting Reading and Writing Rituals

A Bridge to Our Own True Selves

At the end of my junior year at DePaul University, my Black male English professor approached me after class about collaborating on a summer research project. He pitched it as "preparation for post-secondary," his assumption being that I would continue on to some graduate English PhD program. My initial impulse was to say no, noooo thank you, but because I was in my early twenties and disposed to second guessing myself, I accepted his mentorship.

I regretted my choice immediately, but my ambition wouldn't let me recant. Instead, I pushed myself to write a nonrequired thesis to serve as the writing sample for a PhD program to which I had no interest in applying simply because this man, who represented success but whom I actively disliked, suggested I do so.

How could I say no? Here was a professor of color, investing his time and energy in me, my future, an advantage he played weekly: "What you fail to understand, Felicia, is the magnitude of my gesture." Perhaps he was right. As an undergraduate, I lacked the perspective to really see him: vocabulary as crisp as his daily suit and tie, formality an armor from a lifetime of being twice as good to earn half as much. My struggles would not, could not ever, compare to his own—the racial trauma of asserting one's seat among the old guard.

So I baked him snickerdoodles as a commencing thank you gift. He'd make use of this offense over the next several weeks, whenever I least expected: "Perhaps if you'd been less busy playing kitchen," he'd begin, or else snap, "Take your mind off the sweets and stop wasting our time!"

I endured his exasperation with the singular goal of never crying in front of him. That summer I worked hard, and then I worked harder, crafting a survey of La Malinche in early sixteenth- to late twentieth-century literature. Infamous for her role as Hernán Cortés's translator during the Spanish invasion of present-day Mexico City, La Malinche was an Indigenous woman alternately represented as traitor and whore, slave and savant, the mythical mother of the mestizo people. Here was a woman for whom language was a source of power and persecution. Perhaps I chose to study her because she helped me to better understand myself, a Chicana who acquired English but lacked voice. I tortured myself, and my writing, to persuade my professor that I was worth the investment. Use his words, I told myself. Sound like him so that he hears you. Do not fail to understand. Do not fail.

I remember sitting at my desk months earlier as this same professor returned my midterm exam. He taught the English Department's only multicultural literature course—then an elective—by testing students on obscure words scattered throughout three or four novels. I aced the test, having essentially memorized the books. He asked that I stand, and then addressed the class: "Review your scores. If they appear low to you, it's because your classmate here botched the curve." Was his resentment of me personally, I wondered, or my lazy, entitled generation? Because success, on his terms, felt a lot like suffering. Come the final exam, he asked me again to stand. "No," I thought, "noooo thank you, I won't let you humiliate me twice." But then I stood. I stood! Up and out of my seat on command. I felt so stupid, and so powerless, like the good girl that I was.

The feeling was not unfamiliar. Among Chicanx, achievement and ridicule go hand in hand. Growing up, I rarely earned a compliment that wasn't spiked with venom, an effective means of putting me in my place, lest I forgot where I came from: "You think you're white now or what?" Straight A's, an honors award ceremony, reading books outside of school, using "million-dollar words," eating a salad—the scope of the transgression was irrelevant. "Look at you, all fancy. Must be nice." The tone was playful, bitter, self-obsessed: "You think you're better than me?" If I dared to call my family out, they'd just laugh and laugh: "Don't be so sensitive."

I grew up believing that I was defective: overly emotional, hypersensitive, "different." I tried my best to play along, to fit in, to laugh at myself when, really, I hurt. I said what I thought my family wanted to hear, reassurance that I was one of them. Still, I wondered what it might feel like to succeed independent of New Mexico and its poverty and pride. At my high school graduation party, I shared news of my acceptance to Wellesley College with an aunt and uncle. They congratulated me, and then bet that I wouldn't last a year. That one stuck with me. When I transferred to DePaul University sophomore year, I couldn't help but feel that my family had seen through to the real me: uppity, weak, wannabe white, a joke.

This sort of psychological conditioning prepared me well for my professor's brand of mentorship. "It's just the way some people of color are," I thought. Disapproval and public shaming are symptoms of a long-standing cycle of racist abuse. The hardening, the pessimism, ensue from a legacy of survival under a white supremacist capitalist patriarchy. I accommodated his mistreatment of me because I didn't yet believe that I deserved better. Like so many Chicanas before me, I chose obedience (virgin, mother) over self-preservation (traitor, whore), censoring myself to appease a man who couldn't hear me over the sound of his own voice anyway. By the end of that summer, I had systematically substituted my professor's words for my own until I disappeared from the page altogether.

I was twenty or so then. I'd go on to graduate from college, secure a teaching job, earn my MFA. It wasn't until I turned thirty that I was able to clearly articulate my boundaries, to stop translating what I wanted to say into what other people wanted to hear. It took the birth of my son—an enduring postpartum depression, that year-long, aching loneliness, spiked with dread that I was forever trapped by this boy, another male in a long line of males for whom I felt responsible—for me to realize that I was angry. Like, thirty years' worth of enraged, at everyone in my life, past and present, especially myself. For not causing trouble. For playing along. For second-guessing myself. For silencing myself. I can't do this, I told myself, over and over again, breastfeeding in the restaurant bathroom stall so that I didn't embarrass my in-laws, sleeping upright in the wooden rocking chair so that I didn't disturb my son's sleep. And then, one day: I won't do this. It was as simple, as plausible, as "No," spoken from my own authentic voice.

"No," outraged and unapologetic at first, a real rampage, and then, later, tempered with trust in myself, my power.

My impulse as a nonfiction writer is to track the impetus of this evolution, to say that it all started with that summer before my senior year of college, with the project on La Malinche. This isn't true, of course; I'd sensed something was wrong since childhood, but I dedicated years to directing my doubt inward (I'm defective) instead of outward (My culture's kinda messed up). What I can say is that while researching La Malinche, I came across a book called *This Bridge Called My Back: Writings by Radical Women of Color*, a multiracial feminist anthology of poetry and prose that page after page said: "See yourself here, Felicia? What about here?" Gloria Anzaldúa, Cherríe Moraga, and Toni Cade Bambara proved to be my real mentors, modeling how to be a woman of color who commands her own voice.

Donna Kate Rushin, in particular, spoke my name in "The Bridge Poem." She rages against women of color's exhausting intersectional feminism—how race, class, gender, and sexuality compound our oppression. "I've had enough," she starts:

I'm sick of seeing and touching
Both sides of things

Sick of being the damn bridge for everybody. . .
I explain my mother to my father my father to my little sister
My little sister to my brother my brother to the white feminists
The white feminists to the Black church folks the Black church folks
To the ex-hippies the ex-hippies to the Black separatists the
Black separatists to the artists the artists to my friends' parents. . .
Then
I've got to explain myself
To everybody. . .

Her exasperation, her resentment, I felt it, knowing what it is to bend myself at the risk of breaking just to ensure that no one fails to understand: I'm a good girl, pliable and pleasant; I'm a loyal Chicana, not white like you fear; I'm an obedient student, yes, sir; I'm sorry, forgive me, I'll change. "Forget it/I'm sick of it," Rushin declares:

The bridge I must be
Is the bridge to my own power
I must translate
My own fears
Mediate
My own weaknesses
I must be the bridge to nowhere
But my true self
And then
I will be useful[1]

It may have taken years for me to enact the change, but this book, and this poem in particular, reassured me that there was possibility for transformation. I could honor myself *and* my culture; one did not need to negate the other. Once I stopped that damaging legacy of self-denial, I embraced a life of full, courageous, and complex consciousness, both on and off the page.

It's access to this consciousness that fuels our best writing. I'd much rather read raw energy than a writer's practiced attempt to sound like a modern-day Hemingway. "Don't write right," I tell my students, by which I mean, don't torture your words to satisfy the workshop, the workshop leader, or your writing heroes. I say, "Let go of all that. Lose control."

How do we train our workshop participants—many of them young, many of them yet to "find" themselves—to write from an authentic voice?

Peter Elbow talks about the "awkward and sometimes paralyzing translating process in writing."[2] When faced with a blank page, Elbow observes that we all too often stop and ask, "How shall I say this?" It's there—in that moment of self-conscious negotiation—that we translate our words into what we think other people want to hear. Maybe we tend to trip over writing's rules and so we aim for simplicity. Maybe we worry that our attempt will embarrass us and so we aim for safety in ambiguity. Maybe we obsess over the exact right word, sentence by sentence, and so we aim for thesaurus-inspired perfection. The point is, if we're hung up on the reader's experience before we've even written anything, we sacrifice our voice to satisfy someone else.

This habit of trying to control the writing while we write kills the vitality inherent to our authentic voice. Elbow elaborates:

> To write is to overcome a certain resistance: you are trying to wrestle a steer to the ground, to wrestle a snake into a bottle, to overcome a demon that sits in your head. To succeed in writing is to overpower that steer, that snake, that demon. But if, in your struggles to write, you actually break its back, you are in trouble. Yes, now you have power over it, you can say what you need to say, but in transforming that resistant force into a limp noodle, somehow you turn your words into limp noodles, too. Somehow the force that is fighting you is also the force that gives life to your words. . . . This myth explains why some people who write fluently and perhaps even clearly—they say just what they mean in adequate, errorless words—are really hopelessly boring to read. There is no resistance to their words . . . no surprises. The language is too abjectly obedient. When writing is really good, on the other hand, the words themselves lend some of their own energy to the writer.[3]

In order to harness this resistance—that rich, feral creative energy—workshop participants must train in how to write without thinking about writing: how to turn off their internal translator, disobey writing's rules, and channel life back into their words. The goal is mess, aliveness, and a sense of discovery in real time—evidence that participants are thinking and typing in tandem as opposed to stopping and translating word by word. It is writing of the self, for the self.

For writers of color especially, this inward turn offers relief from the burden of obedience, of always having to do and say what other people expect of us. It's a rare opportunity to let loose an authentic voice—not original or groundbreaking, but real—written in the way that we speak. This doesn't mean that workshop participants won't revert back to their usual writing habits when composing a longer project, but it does allow a glimpse of that complex consciousness they're gifted with from birth. Exposure to this power early on means they're one step closer to being bridges to their own true selves.

This chapter focuses on daily reading and writing rituals that draw out participants' authentic voices. First, we bring our bodies into the work, reviving a dynamic definition of workshop that involves mess, mobility, and vulnerability. Next, we break with the habit of reactive writing, aiming for inspired, uncensored energy. Finally, we thwart the impulse to control our text, separating writing, editing, and revision into separate stages of production. The point is power. When participants learn to stop second-guessing themselves and say what they mean, they evolve their writing voices on their own terms.

Reviving Workshop

Students are surprised when they enter my classroom to find baskets of silly putty centered on the tables. "Are these for us?" they ask, delightedly. "Can we touch them?" This simple kinetic experiment—hands and minds in motion—is the first in a series of deviations from the traditional workshop structure, which hinges on a static address: read this and listen to me talk about it, write that and listen to me talk about it. No matter participants' passion for the subject, all that lecturing (from the workshop leader or else a select few peers) will eventually siphon their vital energy. To be alive, you must exercise mobility, engage the senses, and laugh every now and then. I start with silly putty because it brings workshop participants back into their hands, which is where writing enters the world.

For so much of our lives we're schooled into stillness; to fidget is a deficit in absolute attention. I emphasize mindful body language as a sign of respect for fellow workshop participants who read their work aloud; eye contact and poise most certainly matter. But that comes later, in measured periods, so as not to exhaust everyone. Because stillness is exhausting, isn't it? The chronic demand that creative people sit still, keep quiet, and pay attention is more about a teacher's need for control then it is about learning. The old adage of sitting on our hands is an apt metaphor, as narrow-minded educators affirm that doing nothing is preferential to taking action.

The creative writing workshop offers a rare opportunity for dynamic scholarship. To nurture creativity, you have to engender it from the get-go, which means breaking with the traditional workshop's staid, academic formalism and instead opting to revive its industrial origins: a room filled with tools in which artisans tinker, plan, and produce work.

As a graduate student, I wrote some of my best stuff when enrolled in studio art classes. The workshop spaces hummed with creative energy: heaping bins of materials, bodies operating machines, groups of students eating together, sprawled on couches, the floor, talking, collaborating. Everywhere I looked there were strange and colorful projects in process—not private and repressed like my digital Word file, but on full display. This, so different from the silent English building, bereft of writers who siloed in homes, frozen in front of their computer screens.

"Use your hands!" Austin Kleon entreats in his creative guidebook *Steal Like an Artist*. "Art that only comes from the head isn't any good."[4] He elaborates:

Just watch someone at their computer. They're so still, so immo-
bile. You don't need a scientific study (of which there are a few)
to tell you that sitting in front of a computer all day is killing you,
and killing your work. We need to move, to feel like we're making something with our bodies, not just our heads . . . Our nerves
aren't a one-way street—our bodies can tell our brains as much as
our brains tell our bodies. You know that phrase, "going through
the motions"? That's what's so great about creative work: If we
just start going through the motions, if we strum a guitar, or
shuffle sticky notes around a conference table, or start kneading
clay, the motion kickstarts our brains into thinking.[5]

Workshop participants are accustomed to writing as a silent,
solitary, sedentary practice that lends itself to obsession: Did I do it
right? Is it any good? Am I any good? Too many writers are trapped
in this self-doubting headspace. To resuscitate their practice, participants must break free from their heads and reengage with their
bodies as creative instruments.

And so, in my workshops, we use our hands. Participants arrive
to workshop with a composition notebook and pen, with which
they write by hand, every day. I aim to capitalize on the kinetic link
between brain stem, spinal cord, and fingers. Participants feel the
words move across the page. They submit to the physical forward
motion, without stopping, thinking, and correcting. This daily writing ritual targets confidence: to respond, in words, as oneself, trusting that the initial impulse is good enough. Clumsy, messy, raw,
misspelled, disjointed, yes. Perfectly imperfect.

Good enough—bad, even!—is not what participants are accustomed to aiming for as artists, but as they mature in confidence,
they learn that the work must necessarily be "bad" (the attempt)
before it has any chance at being "good" (the vision). I've mentored
talented students who are so frightened of imperfection that they'd
rather not write anything at all. This is why I opt for language like
"workshop draft" and "first draft" over "final draft," as it presumes
there's an ongoing process at play. As Anne Lamott reminds us
in *Bird by Bird*, "Perfectionism is a mean, frozen form of idealism,

while messes are the artist's true friend. . . . We need to make messes in order to find out who we are and why we are here—and, by extension, what we're supposed to be writing."[6] Perfection on the page is a symptom of immobility; participants need to exert energy in order to access authenticity. Make your workshop conducive to mess and watch your writers evolve.

Our daily in-class writing ritual ranges in scope and purpose, and includes:

» Confessionals that detail participants' hopes and fears about writing.

» To-do lists that purge brain clutter by enumerating distracting, non-writing-related obligations and project-related anxieties. Deactivate these thoughts by crumpling the list and tossing it aside.

» Ongoing task lists that prioritize the day's single, most pressing creative focal point.

» Timed freewrites aka "push-ups in withholding judgement" that one, remind participants that writing is a skill that improves with frequency and two, heightens access to images and emotions otherwise inaccessible to the conscious mind.[7]

» Drawings as a creative exercise to brainstorm initial ideas, map out more advanced projects, link disparate memories, and excavate details.

» Guided prompts that generate writing on longer projects so that participants leave workshop with direction.

» Self-reflections in which participants appraise their drafting, workshop, or revision efforts, identify their struggles and successes with a project, and itemize their next moves.

» Guided, in-class micro- and macro-editing sessions to evaluate the strength of their verbs, their reliance on adjectives, adverbs, and cliché, the cadence of their sentences, the complexity of their characters, the vitality of their scenes, and the resonance of their opening and closing paragraphs.

Participants write by hand not just to produce creative work, then, but to teach themselves about the writing process, from initial impulse through the revision stage.

Essential to this writing ritual is that participants stand and share what they wrote aloud, whether it be quick fragments for discussion or whole sections that surprise, move, or trouble them. They'll stumble over their handwriting at first—so unused to seeing their words in print—and apologize for mistakes: missing words, tangents, incomplete thoughts. They'll shirk, shrink, shake, and whisper. This is to be expected, as confidence is a performance that necessitates practice. What's encouraging is how fellow participants are able to see through it all—another writer's mess—and zero in on the most important, poignant elements for discussion.

To be clear, this is not an exercise in critique. Instead, participants respond to a writer's concerns, pointing to compelling insights, images, or energy. In doing so, they help one another get over it and get on with it. It's a real pleasure to witness. Eventually, participants grow more comfortable with their own messy words and more confident in their delivery.

Engaging with the text aloud thwarts perfectionism, demands vulnerability, bolsters trust, and reaffirms that we are, none of us, alone in this writing thing. Most importantly, it celebrates participants' own words, spoken aloud in their unique and powerful voices.

We use our hands, yes, but we also engage our other senses in workshop. Participants listen to music, eat food, doodle in their notebooks or play with silly putty while we listen to an excerpt of a podcast. They move: transitioning between small group workshops and editing stations, standing to read their work aloud, relocating to the hallway to record themselves reading their own work aloud, relocating outside to read a partner's work aloud while the writer listens and takes notes (an exercise that pinpoints when the writing sounds inauthentic: off, false, vague, or wordy). They craft mood boards of early-stage writing projects, visually representing underlying questions and guiding metaphors, which we hang around the classroom. They craft "Family Tree" sculptures that pay homage to their artistic mentors, which we display around the classroom.[8] They print out their pages and then take to the floor, marking sentences with different colored highlighters, cutting up paragraphs and rearranging them on the wall, pasting excerpts from old drafts into the margins of their working draft in order to track personal growth. Workshop isn't workshop if someone doesn't accidentally trip over a writer. While it may take a few extra moments to set up the classroom so that it is conducive to this type of use, those moments are worth the trouble.

A revived definition of workshop necessitates that participants, and their writing, come back to the body, back to life. They touch their creative work, listen to it, reflect on it, see it exhibited on the walls and tables in various stages of production. Never is the work private or perfect, a prisoner of the head. I advocate that workshop participants relinquish control and submit to mess, to good enough, to a personal journey of discovery. To command a pen is to physically grapple with the fact that it is you writing, your voice scrawled on the page, not a rigid Times New Roman facsimile. Workshop participants, thus fully embodied, can risk vulnerability and share of themselves on the page.

Just what are your writers capable of, on their own terms and in their own voices?

Cultivating Inspiration

In this chapter, I speak of participants accessing an authentic voice. That's a loaded term for a lot of people of color. Just how we accomplish "authenticity" depends on the company we keep—it's one way with family, another with friends, and a whole other approach with white folks, who appraise our color, appropriate aspects of our culture, and then critique our performance of race according to their expectations. ("I think of you as white," a white friend once told me, approvingly. A different white friend cautioned me before meeting her family, "Try to tone it down a bit and, you know, fit in.") Authenticity is reactive behavior, similar to the internal translator. We do and say what other people expect of us as evidence of our loyalty. Often, we're not even aware we're doing it, so accustomed are we to the analytical art of code-switching.

This is not the authenticity I'm after.

In this chapter I also speak of participants being real, another loaded term. Often, when people of color demand of one another to stop frontin' and be real, what they're really asking is for the other person to descend an imaginary ladder of socioeconomic status, education, ethics, or pride and return home, to that version of themselves preserved in the memory of friends and family. To be real is to reverse time and distance, another act of self-denial.

That's not what I'm aiming for, either. Participants don't need to prove themselves by sounding some type of way. That's more reactive behavior, a performance to please.

In the context of my workshop, authenticity and realness are a release from all that posturing. A break from being everything to everyone. A ritual of going inward and being present, listening to themselves even when they think they have nothing significant to say. This is what Julia Cameron calls writing from the body: "Dropping down into the well of your experience and sounding out how you feel," thus acquiring "the same resonance that a singer does when the breath comes from the diaphragm rather than high up in the chest."[9] The writing is by them, for them, because the impulse to create came from within them.

How do you achieve inspiration in your workshop?

The first step is to resist reactive writing assignments, those token exercises in which students read a model text and then imitate the often white, male writer (see the introduction). This positions participants to sound like someone else before they've even explored what it is to sound like themselves! Instead, consider assignments that open participants up to their own potential.

I ask my workshop participants to make a list of reasons why it is important for them to tell the truth about their lives. I ask them to make a list of reasons why their writing is powerful. I ask them to complete the phrase "I give myself permission to _____," so as to offer release. I ask them to enumerate ten things that currently inspire them and then pick one as their homework assignment. I ask them to freewrite about what they're exploring, and then later freewrite about what they've found. I ask them to complete the phrase "I am growing into _____" as a reminder that they're growing, we all are, every day.

It's hard to create from a place of inspiration when participants are forcing it, knocking out assignments on autopilot, and so I begin workshop with a quick self-assessment: You've committed to this class, but are you willing to make the time and space for inspiration in your day-to-day life?

» Write out your schedule for this term. Set it aside.

» Write about a time when you felt completely inspired—something that really stands out in your memory. What about that experience inspired you? What were the circumstances?

» Make a list of times that ideas come to you.

» Investigate your list for a pattern. Are you relaxed? Are you doing something else (like driving or showering or exercising or talking)?

» Once you've figured out what your list has in common, brainstorm how to incorporate more of that kind of activity in your day. Learn how your mind works and then feed it when it is most productive.

» What things leave you feeling unmotivated or sap your energy? Make a list.

» Is it possible to lessen or eliminate any items on your list, at least temporarily?

» Return to your schedule. How can you simplify your life so that you have more time to feel inspired and make art?

Participants assess their responsibilities over the course of the workshop, delineating between their obligations to others (employers, professors, volunteer work, student organizations, roommates, family, partners, and friends) and their obligations to themselves (spiritual devotion, creative work, physical health, mental health, and relaxation). So often these lists skew toward satisfying others, evidence that we spend the best part of our day negating our own needs. When we're finally free for "me time," our energy's down, our brains slow—we're wasted. How can we possibly write in that state?

The choice is theirs: commit to their creative work as a priority, or don't. Sometimes participants panic at the sight of their obligations laid bare on the page. Sometimes I panic at the sight of their obligations laid bare on the page! They end up dropping the workshop, and that's okay; they're not yet ready to sacrifice for their creative work. The remaining participants round out their self-assessment by scheduling daily opportunities for inspiration, like mini-dates with themselves. When are they at their best, energy-wise? How can they harness that energy into their creative work? This may mean quitting a commitment, waking up earlier, swapping work shifts, or shutting down a toxic relationship—a powerful outcome that I hadn't anticipated when creating this exercise. Participants concede that it's okay to put themselves first, to claim a time and space for writing that best serves them. This is the groundwork for claiming an authentic voice.

Now that there's room for inspiration, I assign daily out-of-class writing exercises for the first few weeks of workshop, akin to two-a-day football practices before the high school season started. Creative conditioning, if you will. Unlike the traditional writing workshop, which requires participants to create one or maybe two polished drafts per term, I advocate writing (and reading work aloud) as often as possible in order to train participants to release control and submit to inspiration.

This is a strategy that author Gretchen Rubin calls "harnessing the power of frequency."[10] Rubin explains that it's easier to write when the pressure to be brilliant is off. No one day's work is exemplary of who she is as a writer; if something doesn't work out, she moves on to a different approach. "My consequent lack of anxiety," admits Rubin, "puts me in a more playful frame of mind and allows me to experiment and take risks."[11] It's this early freedom to mess up, to make messes, that brings about a rewarding boldness in participants' work.

Rubin cites other benefits to frequency, including a quicker start time (when writing is ingrained as a habit, so is the momentum to make work—suddenly a blank page is less daunting), the ability to get out of her head and just say it (enabling more productive writing in a shorter span of time), a guarantee of progress (there's no need to despair over not writing), and that magical, Matrix-like state of mind that results from consistent creative output (suddenly everything feels related to the work). In my experience, frequency teaches workshop participants that writing is less a high-stakes assignment dictated by the workshop leader, and more an instinctive impulse to create. The more we nurture this impulse at the beginning of workshop, the more likely it is to stick. The goal is for participants to embrace writing as a daily creative ritual—it's just something that they do, without us having to tell them to do it.

Some daily out-of-class writing exercises vary, and include:

Writer's Notebook: This is where participants' ideas take shape. It's an uncensored, spontaneous dialogue with themselves, holding the subjects and ideas they intend to write about as well as the stuff they're actually writing about. It holds a lot of odds and ends, too—brainstorms and dialogue and lists and images and drawings and quotes.

Freewriting Prompts: Timed freewriting is practice in keeping our hand in motion and our mind open to the words. Each participant receives a sealed envelope containing two or more prompts, printed on separate slips of paper. Participants return home with their envelopes, from which they blindly select one prompt. With a timer handy, they write by hand without stopping for five minutes and then repeat until the envelope is empty.

Exquisite Corpse: Participants play this game of consequences in teams to build community and develop quick decision-making skills. Every student has one hour to divine inspiration from and contribute to their team's exquisite corpse. The only way to "win" is to trust their gut instincts. I place a binder clip, a blank composition notebook, and an art object (a children's picture book, perhaps, or a tarot card, or song lyrics) into a manila envelope. Participants sign up for a one hour writing shift ranging from directly after class into the late evening, making note of the teammates proceeding and following them. Writer #1 selects a manila envelope, retreats to a private work-space, studies its contents for inspiration, and then crafts a creative response, handwritten in the composition notebook. When fin-ished, Writer #1 advances to the next blank page and neatly prints their last line on the top of the page. This line serves as the prompt for Writer #2. Writer #1 then binder clips the pages so that the note-book opens directly to the prompt. At the end of the hour, Writer #1 meets Writer #2 to exchange the comp notebook. The process repeats until the entire team has participated.

Weekend Playlist: The playlist encourages participants to break with routine and access inspiration from outside of themselves. I assign a visit to a local gallery, science museum, or contemporary art muse-um; a pleasure read; a documentary film; an hour-long walk; and a drawing exercise. Participants then write for thirty minutes in their Writer's Notebook.

Call and Response: This is an opportunity to pay tribute to the artistic talent in our classroom. Participants choose a compelling line, image, character, etc., from a classmate's work and use it as inspiration for their own creative exercise.

Whatever the prompt, the point is that participants reserve time in their day to nurture the creative impulse: to tune in, open up, and write from a nonjudgmental place of inspiration. With fre-quent opportunity to fail, play, and experiment, they train their authentic voice to flex on command.

Beyond guided exercises, I think it's important to expose participants to my own rituals as writer. Once a week, on Fridays, I e-mail participants a quick "mixtape" of five online links. Maybe it's a new album, an episode of a television show or podcast, a magazine article, a comic—whatever hodgepodge media I came across that week that I found particularly compelling. These e-mails are not mandatory reading. They're a gesture of comradery: I'm a writer, too; I have to excavate inspiration from my daily life just like you. .

This extends into the classroom, where I hang a clothesline across one wall. When I find an inspiring image, text, or quote, I pin it to the line. The clothesline is not something I comment on, it's just there, available for whomever to browse. Mostly it serves as a colorful reminder of my own purpose on the page. Soon enough, one by one, more objects appear on the clothesline as students anonymously share their own sources of inspiration.

Creativity is a commitment, a habit, a lifestyle. When we tap into our full creative selves, we are authentic and real, without having to expand or contract on demand: more Chicana, less Oreo, more feminine, less feminist. What a relief to turn inward and reassure ourselves that we're enough exactly as we are! When we trust that we can do no wrong, the words come easier.

Relinquishing Control

When I assign a prompt—a timed ten-minute freewriting session, say—I clarify that all ten minutes are meant for writing: a nonstop, plow ahead, messy release of words, rife with error. That's hard work, censoring the internal translator, and hard on the hand, too. After a week's practice in letting go, I build on this prompt, adding a follow-up ten-minute session dedicated exclusively to editing in the tradition of Peter Elbow's quick-revising process.[12] During the editing session, participants may reread their work, correct surface mistakes such as missing words or misspellings, tweak phrases to their liking, cross others out, and add in additional material here and there. There's no scrapping the lot and starting again, just quick copyediting for clarity.

The key is that the two stages, writing and editing, release and control, are separate; one is not intrinsic to the other. Too often when participants "write," they spend the majority of their time editing: staring at the screen, thinking, writing a word and then immediately rereading it or deleting it or hating it or replacing it or second-guessing its fit. The balance is distorted; participants create from a place of despair, judgment, and fear. By timing the editing session, I aim to cut down on participants' propensity for self-loathing. The ritual restores balance: writing and editing are of equal weight, completed to the best of participants' abilities in the allotted amount of time. The goal is good enough, a gesture of self-acceptance.

Susan Bell, author of *The Artful Edit: On the Practice of Editing Yourself*, teaches, "To edit is to listen, above all; to hear past the emotional filters that distort the sound of our all too human words; and to then make choices rather than judgments."[13] When participants write from fear, they are incapable of hearing anything beyond their own vulnerability. To put an ear to the page and listen feels like unwelcome exposure. They'd rather get it perfect the first time so as to convince themselves and the workshop that they're invincible, not clumsy human hands and heart, but a superhuman writer of the mind. What they don't realize is that the headspace is no good for creative writing, too close-quartered to engender growth.

How do you teach your workshop participants to make choices about their work, rather than judgments? Distinguish between writing, editing, and revision as separate stages of creative production. Likely your workshop participants have been trained to conflate the separate skills of writing and editing, and confuse revision with a rote checklist of things to fix so as to earn the workshop leader's approval. Yet creation and craft are skillsets that require separate tools. Participants can't apply these tools if they don't have access to them. The traditional workshop leader certainly won't lend them out, choosing instead to wield editing and revision strategies as authoritative prowess: change this, move that, delete here, see? Participants do as they're told, even if it detracts from their artistic vision, because they're bottom of the workshop hierarchy. What do they know? So accustomed to judging their own work, they're quick to accept the judgement of the workshop leader.

Try putting the tools in their hands. Teach your workshop participants to create from a place of fearlessness, to hear past the emotional filters (This isn't any good, you're not any good) and instead make steady choices about their work.

Our three-stage creative production includes the following reflective prompts:

Writing: Writing is listening to our work first with humility and love—really hearing the sound of our own voice, deep from the diaphragm. We release uninhibited energy, then read the words aloud. We ask ourselves, "How did the writing feel? What did I learn from the attempt?"

Editing: Editing is listening to our work with perspective and intention, clearing the grounds for a more focused read. We revisit our initial attempt and ask, "What energy, image, line, or idea would I like to pursue here? How can I employ my mechanical writing skills to best showcase that pursuit in the allotted amount of time? Recognizing that the work is not yet fully realized, how can I communicate my vision to my fellow workshop participants so as to elicit their pointed guidance?"

Revision: Revision is listening to our work with a detached critical consciousness in order to hear "what the words don't yet say, but want to say."[14] We return to our workshop draft and read it aloud. Then we ask, What was my initial vision for the work, and how does that differ from what I've created here? What is my present vision? How might I "re-see" my draft so that it more closely aligns with my present vision? What is my plan of action so that the parts of my draft make for a more cohesive whole? Recognizing that the work is not yet fully realized, how can I embrace this revised draft as my best effort to date?

The three-stage ritual establishes distance between writing, editing, and revision tasks, enabling participants to engage with their work less out of despair, judgment, and fear, and more from a levelheaded, tactical perspective. Participants learn to assess—and accept—their writing in phases.

Providing your workshop participants with the tools they need to evolve their writing on their own terms means you're teaching them how to listen to themselves. This is the power of self-awareness, that instinctive trust in their own complex consciousness. Such self-awareness serves your writers of color well. They learn to relinquish control of the mind in favor of the body, accept themselves as they are, and mature into their authentic voices. With practice, they're equipped with the metacognition necessary to name and apply their craft choices by themselves, for themselves.

A former workshop participant reflects:

> When I first walked into class, I hadn't written anything creative in months, hadn't written anything on paper with a pen in a year, and I was feeling overwhelmed at the prospect of doing either of those things. My free-writes reflect that. The first pieces are covered in scribbled out phrases. Nothing I wrote was good enough to occupy space on the page. But slowly I found a sense of peace from the process. It became a ritual: sit down, pen to paper, breathe. I stopped censoring. I learned that yes, true to my worst fears, I will write things that are trite, and boring, and confusing, and that's okay. And I learned that if I let myself write those things, and dig deeper, and be brave, something magical will happen: I will start to create hard and true and beautiful things. And that's a feeling that never loses its shine.

Mentorship in the New Millennium

It's no secret that college and university faculty of color—especially junior, female-identifying faculty of color—mentor a disproportionate number of students. This is in addition to a full teaching load, departmental meetings, committee meetings, advisees, our own research, and the obligations of home life. There's little time to pivot between commitments; some days just showing up feels like a success. Still, we have to show up. Our skin tone is so highly visible, everyone sees our absence. And so we push ourselves to attend, push ourselves to respond on matters of diversity, our presumed specialism. We push ourselves to check our anger, act approachable, smile. Never mind the handful of microaggressions we endured between the parking lot and the elevator. Our professional advancement depends on our willingness to perform, doing and saying the right thing on command. The emotional and psychological violence of our labor is unceasing.

When we return to our offices—physically, mentally, and emotionally fatigued—to find a student of color standing outside our door, how do we respond?

"Do you have a minute?" the student asks.

Our impulse is to say no (I have papers to grade, a salad to eat, a class to teach, a psyche to protect) which translates to, "Yes, of course! Come on in. What's on your mind?"

When I think of my professor all those years ago, I wonder what he held back in our exchanges. When he ridiculed my test scores, my snickerdoodles, my writing, what was he really raging against?

It wasn't me. I know that now.

Shampa Biswas, author of "Advice on Advising: How to Mentor Your Minority Students," admits, "Graduate school doesn't teach you advising skills. Mostly you model your mentors. Like most faculty members I had to learn how to advise on the job."[15] This strategy of modeling your mentors on the fly might very well contribute to a cycle of abuse among people of color. Old school merits of stoicism, authoritarianism, and tough love don't cut it anymore. Today's students expect our camaraderie. They claim unrestricted access to our time, e-mailing and conferencing for reassurance of their talent, resources for their activism, and guidance on their intimate personal lives. And students of color? By the time they reach out, they're desperate.

"Do you have a minute?" the student asks.

It's up to us to kill the smile, cut the performance, and respond with an authentic voice.

"If all you do is respond with the sort of assimilative language of 'inclusivity' that has taken over higher education, that's not going to help these students feel like valuable members of the campus," writes Biwas. "What will help: treating their concerns as valid critiques that require a personal, departmental, or institutional response."[16] This may mean addressing the campus culture head-on by assisting the student on an e-mail, news article, petition, or formal complaint. It may mean speaking on the student's behalf in a faculty meeting. It may mean sitting in silence with the student, commiserating on institutional racism at large. And it may mean calling the student out when they fail to understand the magnitude of your gesture.

Listen mindfully. By doing so, you teach the student to listen to themselves. This is what it is to be self-aware.

Talk candidly. By doing so, you teach the student to talk, too. This is what it is to be vulnerable.

And say no when you need to say no. By doing so, you teach the student to disobey a cultural imperative to please. This is what it is to exercise self-preservation.

Enough with this legacy of self-denial. Mentor your students in how to command their own voices.

CHAPTER FOUR

Completing the Canon

A New Normal

In Chicago, I had the opportunity to take a fiction writing workshop with Ana Castillo (or The Ana Castillo, as I referred to her, author of *So Far from God*, *Peel My Love Like an Onion*, and *I Ask the Impossible*—copies of which I cradled in my arms that first night of class in hopes of securing her signature). She was Chicanisma in the flesh: Wide-brimmed ranchero hat and squash blossom necklace, regal posture, an unapologetic refusal to smile. Her whole vibe said don't fuck with me, and God, how I admired that, the rejection it entailed, polar opposite to my desire for acceptance.

Instead of the usual introductions, she began workshop with a question.

"What do you hate?" she asked.

"What do we hate?" someone echoed.

"What do you hate?" she repeated, to stunned silence.

As much as I wanted to please her with an answer, I couldn't respond. No one had ever asked me this question before, at least not out loud. The answers were always assumed among people of color, a sideways flick of the eyes that said oh hell no, a squeeze of the hand that said it's not worth it, a steely gaze that said choose wisely now. I was a young, working-class woman of color fighting to earn an education in a white supremacist capitalist patriarchy. What didn't I hate? Men's opinions of my body on the walk to the train station, exposés on Abu Ghraib torture in the newspaper dispenser, my obligatory negotiation between a transit pass or grocery money, the brown line train's scenic transformation from dilapidated brick and Cheeto trash to trimmed lawns and Dominick's Grocery, the white classmate who announced that racism isn't a thing anymore.

Hate? I was the only workshop participant of color in the room. I couldn't—I wouldn't respond.

Finally, a white male student in the back yelled, "Capri pants!"

Ana Castillo nodded her head once, hesitated, and then wrote "capri pants" on the whiteboard.

"And those fluffy Ewok-looking boots," said someone else.

Ana Castillo wrote "fluffy boots" on the whiteboard.

"Don't you guys hate those new fat-free chocolate chip muffins in the Student Center?"

Ana Castillo opened her mouth as if to speak, but then turned and wrote "muffins" on the whiteboard.

"You know what I like, really, really hate?" said a white female student. "Kelly Clarkson." The group laughed.

"What. What?" stammered Ana Castillo. "Kelly who?"

"She's a singer from American Idol," said the student. "Be grateful you don't know who she is."

"But I asked you what you hate! What about genocide? What about AIDS? What about rape?"

In the silence that followed, I felt the mood plummet from play-ful levity to put-on earnestness, a conciliatory oh-she-wants-us-to-be-political pretense. We collectively became Very Serious Students, because of course genocide, unquestionably yes, and AIDS, and rape, my goodness.

"Us," I wanted to say. "I hate all of us." I hate that you white people get to talk about muffins first and fear second. And I hate that I'm so goddamn afraid of your response to my own daily fear that I don't talk at all.

To be clear, "normal" workshop is muffins. Muffins and boots and other quirky everyday (white, middle-class, heteronormative) details that "breathe life into the work." Normal workshop caters to (white) creativity, (white) imagination, and (white) autonomy on the page, safeguarding "pure art" from the thorny nuisance of politics. Claudia Rankine observes:

> Certain life experiences are said to belong to sociology and not to poetry. . . . To write beyond the white imagination's notion of normality and normality's traumas is to write "political poetry," "sociology," "identity politics poetry," "protest poetry,"—many labels but none of them Poetry. For in order for poetry to be poetry white readers must find it relatable and only then can it transcend its unrelatable 'nonwhite' writer.[1]

The dichotomy is tired: Pure art or political art. Muffins or genocide.

When Ana Castillo began class with a discussion of hate rooted in her own experience—effectively dismissing students' vantage points as frivolous—she transgressed the boundaries of white normality, flagging a deviation from normal workshop to Other, a special elective that accommodates not only race but also gender, class, and sexuality. In other words, a special elective that accommodates a "nonwhite" normal, for indignity, pain, rage, and trauma are so rooted in the psyches of people of color that when someone straight up asks us about it (What do you hate?), we shrug (Do you even need to ask?).

As evidenced by the Other designation, white workshop participants can choose whether or not to occupy this "nonwhite" normal. Academia thus pits whiteness as antithetical to "nonwhiteness": "This is Creative Writing, not Ethnic Studies! What a downer, to be a Very Serious Student. Better, perhaps, to stick with normal workshop, that 'fundamental' class dedicated to 'pure art,' 'real craft.'" Dedicated, most pointedly, to the Western literary canon, that paragon of white imagination.

By definition, canon conjures sacred rule, authoritative law, a timeless norm by which we judge taste and culture. In his 2007 anthology *Literary Genius*, editor Joseph Epstein appoints twenty-five "classic" writers as definitive of Western literature. The list features twenty-two white men and three white women. "Not a very politically correct selection," he admits in his introduction, but to have included other writers "would have opened the gates too widely."[2] Indeed. To uphold canonical purity, one must limit oneself to only the most inspired (white, nearly exclusively male) minds.

Don't be fooled, Rankine warns: ". . .white civility, intelligence, and imagination, and beauty included having slaves, building reservations and internment camps, lynching people, withholding the right to vote and incarcerating large segments of our nonwhite population."[3] Viewed as such, the white imagination is profoundly political, always has been. Whiteness isn't antithetical to "nonwhiteness"; it's contingent on it. Creative Writing is Ethnic Studies is Gender and Sexuality Studies is Political Science is Religion is History is Sociology. The dichotomy is a sham: All art is political art. Anything less is denial. Denial being the most political choice of all: to elect out, to not bear witness, to laugh about muffins knowing, all the while, that your nonaction exonerates hate.

And yet traditional workshop leaders yield to denial, exalting white authors and their protagonists as superior, safeguarding them in expensive, anthologized tomes that people of color must read and discuss and imitate and memorize and recite and pore over line by line on every single literacy test from elementary school to graduate school. There's nothing harmful about the texts themselves, of course, assuming they're analyzed in a multidimensional context. What *is* harmful is workshop leaders' collective hallucination of white universality that situates people of color as abnormal.

Austin Channing Brown, author of *I'm Still Here: Black Dignity in a World Made for Whiteness*, puts it well: "It can be dangerous for Black women to attempt to carve out space for themselves . . . in places that haven't examined the prevailing assumption of white culture. The danger of letting whiteness walk off with our joy, our peace, our sense of dignity and self-love, is ever present."[4] Brown centers her argument around Black women, but I believe the same holds true for many other people of color. To lose oneself in a book takes on new meaning.

Dangerous, too, to jostle the white dream state awake, for denial conjures guilt. (Here the rebuttal "But all lives matter!" comes to mind.) To call attention to the canon's hegemony is to solicit workshop leaders' righteous outrage, bewilderment, defensiveness, annoyance, and dismissal—the same old shields against a multiracial reality.

Is white artistic autonomy supposed to stoop to people of color's survival?

Must art's politics be correct?

Why, yes, if correct means complete. For when else in academia do we strive to be incorrect?

Incorrect workshop leaders teach their students of color to gaze through a lens of whiteness in order to access "the human element."

Incorrect workshop leaders teach their students of color to endorse racist representations of themselves as accurate, inconsequential, representative of a bygone era, or beside the point.

Incorrect workshop leaders teach their students of color to mimic whiteness in order to "access their voice."

Incorrect workshop leaders teach their students of color to read and write by cleaving their consciousness in two, prioritizing the normal, white perspective above their own, abnormal, perspective.

It's time to come correct. Enough with the denial. Let's fling open the gates and step aside.

"Leaving it to chance and throwing up hands in exasperation when it comes to diversity just won't do any more," writes author and University of California, Los Angeles, professor Fred D'Aguiar, "since to surrender rather than to embrace reform risks a process of atrophy of the institutional imagination in a testing economic and social climate when there is urgent need to grow and be flexible."[5]

Growth is urgent because creative writing MFA programs are under fire for lack of resourcefulness. Dwindling affordability, outmoded course offerings ("hybrid" being the buzzword of late), and racial tokenism compromise their appeal.[6] Why risk atrophy? Creative writing's institutional imagination is muscled by the minds of our great contemporary writers! Lord knows it's harder than ever to secure a tenure-track teaching position without proof of artistic ingenuity. If creative writing professors put that ingenuity into practice, MFA programs could lead the pack in progressive reform, advancing cutting-edge curriculum that attracts multicultural faculty and students alike.

But no. The same writers who demand freedom on the page can't seem to care about their program's white tyranny. "Writers in the role of administrators become odd arbiters of taste by paying minimal attention to inclusion as a gateway to a diverse student body," comments D'Aguiar. He continues:

> On one level, the radical imagination thrives outside of teaching time. On another, the most conservative responses from writers are on display during term time as if that radical is reserved for the real enterprise of writing while teaching must suffer slings and arrows of blind conformity and dispiriting bias. It's wrong to separate the two as private and public.[7]

For institutions like university MFA programs, to correct art's politics—to complete the canon—to recruit, recognize, and respect faculty and students of color—is seemingly not worth the public display of energy. The unspoken implication is that if white people don't stand to gain from the inclusion of people of color, there is no need to bother. It's easier to subsidize denial as status quo with a winded, "What more can we do?"

Writing faculty who refuse to flex their imaginations around a multiracial reality are complicit in the fabrication of racism, for their apathy serves to maintain white supremacy. The trajectory is tricky: First they bar a nonwhite normal as outside the boundaries of art. Then they bar a nonwhite person as outside the boundaries of the art academy. When confronted with evidence of bias, they duck out, wielding denial as shield.

How, then, do we move from passivity to progress?

We anti-racist workshop leaders choose to do it ourselves, inside and outside of the academy, without permission. We reject the academy as a system of white-centered control. We take pedagogical cues from organizations like Callaloo and #teachlivingpoets to reject the Western literary canon as a system of suppression. We choose instead to create a new power dynamic.

Activist DeRay McKesson says it straight: " . . . our goal as people of color is never to become white; that is, it is never to extend the idea of domination, but rather to change the conception of power itself."[8] Alongside white accomplices,[9] we must choose to correct art's politics from domination to inclusion. Only then can we escape the danger of losing our dignity to literacy. The work is a matter of survival. "It is a different type of work to survive whiteness," reflects McKesson. "To challenge it, to escape its grasp, and to love oneself in spite of it—this is the work of people of color."[10]

This chapter posits a system of choices that promote justice, dignity, and self-love in the creative writing classroom. Workshop leaders supplement participants' own writing with a living archive of scanned print material, sourced pdfs, and multimedia art by young people, people of color, women, queer, differently abled, and gender-nonconforming artists. Accessible online, this living archive exposes participants to POC-friendly publishing platforms, multimedia art, and experimental genres. Most crucially, it allows for conversation with the authors themselves, contextualizing the texts within specific lived experiences. The ultimate goal is to invest in our collective integrity by renouncing white universality. Together, we can complete the cannon and create a new normal.

Confidence Begins in the Body

As a rule of practice, I do not begin workshop with model texts that instruct participants in how to write a story, poem, scene, or essay. Instead, we just write. And vent, and risk-take, and confess our fears, and riff off one another, and most of all wander. When that freedom to put words on the page shifts from panic to habit—participants' pens fly during freewrites, they stand taller when reading their work aloud, they stop apologizing so much, they don't come to me as often with fears of doing it wrong—that's when I know that we're ready to move on to a study of craft (a topic I cover in depth in chapter 5).

It's important that my workshop participants demonstrate confidence first and technical proficiency second. Writing is a relationship with the self, after all. It's a ritual of tuning in and listening to the language inside of us. Those words are power. Power to make sense of ourselves, by ourselves, independent of the system of white supremacy that tells people of color that we have no dignity, no history, no art, no voice.

Confidence says, "I exist; you cannot erase me."

We dare to tune in and listen to our own words, in our own tongues, and translate them onto the page with our own fists. We stand and read our work aloud in our own voices. We reveal a past and a future nurtured by our own artistic mentors. We claim names for ourselves and demand that everyone calls us by our names. In claiming names for ourselves, we name that for which we fight.

These are writing's real roots.

Institutionalized literacy has always been a means to preserve white dominance. From anti-educational slave codes to Indian boarding schools, Jim Crow laws to English-only mandates, racially motivated school zoning regulations to SAT and GRE testing, those in power exploit the rules of reading and writing in an effort to dehumanize, pacify, assimilate, and control people of color. But storytelling signals liberation, a reclaiming of our collective humanity, our joy and our sorrow, our intellect and our wit. Storytelling is an age-old impulse passed down between generations. Our stories are our passage, a means of continuity with places and people long past, as well as a way forward. They're stored in the body, that un-colonized place of spirit, song, and dance. Cherríe Moraga explains:

> The very act of writing, then, conjuring/coming to "see" what has yet to be recorded in history, is to bring into consciousness what only the body knows to be true. The body—that site which houses the intuitive, the unspoken, the viscera of our being—this is the revolutionary promise of "theory in the flesh": for it is both the expression of evolving political consciousness and the

creator of consciousness itself. Seldom recorded and
ored, our theory incarnate provides the most relia
to liberation.[11]

And so, I begin with the body—writing by hand, without the aid
of a model text—instead of the mind. The trained mind is quick to
submit to convention for the sake of survival: What do you want me
to say, and how do you want me to say it? The body is where liberation lives. To call up our words is an act of justice. To honor them on
the page is an act of dignity. To read them aloud is an act of self-love.

Our workshop participants, then, are the first step toward completing the canon. Teach them to listen to themselves, to one other,
to use storytelling as a means to define what change sounds like. Ask
them: What do you hate? Where are you from? What gives you hope?

Modernizing the Anthology

As an undergraduate, I couldn't afford the required anthologies for
my core English classes, and so I would scramble across the city from
public library to public library until I secured an approximation of
what I needed. The professor's assigned page numbers never corre-
sponded to my texts, being that my borrowed editions were years out
of date, but I'd make do. When the library failed me, I'd buy the text
from the bookstore, commit to a hot afternoon at the photocopier,
and painstakingly steal the pages of each reading listed on the syllabus before returning the book and recouping my money.

The panic I felt at affording my literacy was real. The shame,
too. My library book covers stood out as different, wrong. I internalized the conspicuousness of not looking "normal," yet again.

When I transitioned into the role of teaching assistant at the
University of New Mexico, I promised to put my course texts on
reserve at the university library in advance, as well as stock two or
three extra copies in my office to loan out to students. As it turned
out, I never made good on that promise. By the time I was in a position to design my own syllabi, my definition of "anthology" had

shifted from the traditional Norton to a curated course packet of my favorite texts, photocopied and bound by binder clip, showcasing historical and contemporary writers of color.

Troublesome to think that the pressures of convention were once so gripping, but it took a conscious risk to deviate from "our cherished writers" to my cherished writers, at least at the undergraduate level. During my years previous, teaching Chicago high school students, I hadn't thought twice about assigning writers of color, but being back on a college campus evoked a long-suppressed anxiety that made me, and my choices, feel taboo. In the end, I thought, "Screw it. My classroom, my choice."

Of course, I had to defend those choices to my supervisor and a select few teaching assistants in my cohort, who argued that by deviating from the "classic" curriculum—white male authors and the traditional five-paragraph essay—I deprived students of cultural capital. Whose culture, I wondered? I taught two sections of twenty-five or so first-year students, a significant percentage of whom were Latino, Native, and biracial. To hear my supervisor tell it, by investing in my students' respective cultures, I posed to sabotage their social mobility (the implication being that nonwhite students needed the advantage of white literacy to qualify as educated). To read narratives by writers of color might hurt students of color, you know, in the long run.

These arguments deeply concerned me. If my students were majority white, would we be fretting over their access to cultural capital? None of us are exonerated from the responsibility of exposing students to writers of color, regardless of our classroom's racial and ethnic composition.

The English Department's emphasis on cultural capital meant that first sequential link—English 101—was another cog in the mechanism of white supremacy. My classroom, my choice, felt like a ruse. Still, I refused to replicate a system of study that subjugated people of color. I listened to my colleagues' concerns, but moved forward with my own approach, trusting that my students could draw on their decades-long secondary study of white authors to accommodate future college work. Until then, we focused on first accessing our own voices, writing and recording This-I-Believe essays, before supplementing with the course packet of historical and contemporary writers of color. While this explicit study of writers of color was nowhere near enough of a counterbalance to complete students' literary cultural education or to make up for the deficit that teaching only white writers, domestically and globally, creates, it was an early attempt at completing the canon.

Two years later—this time I was teaching at the University of Iowa—I was again planted at the photocopier, preparing a course packet for my Introduction to Creative Nonfiction class. An undergraduate whom I didn't know interrupted the hypnotic drone and flash to ask if I'd ever considered distributing a digital course packet, "to help save the Earth." Truth was, I hadn't; having grown up analog, the tangible just felt right. The weight, the smell, the sound of pages flipping between my fingertips, all evoked learning. Talk about taboo! Take away the book, then take away the paper? The more I thought about it, though, digitizing my anthology would allow workshop participants access to a range of multimedia works that otherwise did not translate to the page. An added bonus, it would eliminate the cost of materials, and consequently the financial burden on low-income students. "Screw it," I thought. "It's worth trying."

My second iteration of the anthology, then, was a dynamic living archive of PDFs by historical and contemporary writers of color, women, queer, differently abled, and gender-nonconforming artists, interspersed with electronic links to photo essays, graphic essays, spoken word poetry recordings, stand-up comedy, audio essays, video essays, and a hip-hop album. Whereas before I worried about breaking convention, this time I aimed for defiance, unapologetically curating my twenty-first-century take on creative nonfiction.

When I posted this living archive to my course page on the university's learning management system, the material felt unwieldly. Inherent to digital scholarship is its unboundedness. To progress through the works linearly, as one would a course packet, seemed counterintuitive. I needed a means of organizing my material so that

it read as both accessible and integrated, without resorting to a ge-
neric breakdown of genre (that old read this/write that model of
imitation). I certainly didn't intend for my workshop participants
to produce work in every genre; instead, I hoped to broaden their
definition of the essay beyond "timeless" works by canonical writers.

The time is now, I thought. What are folks up to now?

In the end, I chose to organize my living archive by craft element: voice, imagery, characterization, and arrangement (what students call "flow"). I designated five or six essays per craft element.
In doing so, I hoped to synthesize my selections. An audio essay
aside a graphic essay aside a lyric essay—it all came down to a conversation of craft over content. No matter if you liked or disliked
the writing. No matter if you related to the author's experience.
The questions that guided discussion were: Where and how did the
essays exhibit voice? Now, from your observations, what is voice,
to you? All students could participate in the conversation, seeing
as the multimodal selections appealed to diverse learning styles.
What's more, I could tailor selections to each workshop participant, suggesting readings that spoke to their individual aesthetic.

Again, my colleagues had questions. By dabbling in such a
broad range of genres, didn't I ultimately limit students' understanding of the essay? By which they meant, limit students' understanding of the traditional essay, located on the page, traced from a
historical context of white authors. By which they meant, limit the
cultural capital dog-eared for white space. I argued that my focus
was less on teaching students the essay, and more on teaching students how to essay, both on and off the page. By equipping them
with choice (students selected their own preferred readings from
each category), and with craft (students collectively defined a rubric
of craft elements based on their readings), and with the freedom to
risk-take (students exhibited craft by experimenting across genres of
their choosing), they demonstrated curiosity, inquiry, and a journey
of thinking that in and of itself was essayistic.

My definition of anthology deepened when I transitioned to
Colorado College. Almost a decade had passed between my stint at

the University of New Mexico—that young woman at the photocopier, preserving her cherished writers of color—to now, when writers
of color are seemingly everywhere online (read: from nothing to
something) thanks to a push from alternative, digital publishing
venues (#resistance). Even multimedia writing was commonplace, a
catchphrase I no longer had to explain to my English Department
coworkers. My resources richened, and as a result, I was able to
forge ahead with another test of convention.

What if I retired my historical writers of color, and showcased
only contemporary writers of color, women, queer, differently abled,
and gender-nonconforming artists? What if, in that showcase, I
chose to prioritize young writers? What if those young writers featured in progressive online literary journals whose mission was to
promote POC voices?

Screw it, right?

At this point in my career, I was a Visiting Assistant Professor
of English, endowed with a two-year, postgraduate research fellowship. In other words, I was the academic equivalent of a temp, so
departmental colleagues pretty much left me to my own devices.
No longer distracted by the extra work of neutralizing alarm over
cultural capital, I could devote my full energy to correcting art's
politics. My living archive transformed into an inclusive learning
tool. Workshop participants saw themselves reflected in the selection of young writers, empowering them to claim the identity of
author. They left class equipped with a database of potential publishing venues that valued their voices (and many of them went on
to publish). And they gleaned inspiration from writers of color, the
new norm.

In response, participants began to open up, seeking me out after class with, "This reminds me of . . ." or "Have you ever heard of
. . .". Of course, I hadn't heard, so I started a running list of their artistic mentors. That's when it hit me. Here I was, so emphatic about
completing the canon, and yet in being the only decision-maker I
was replicating the same system of power that valued domination
over inclusion. It was me who appointed the Literary Geniuses, me

who guarded the gate. Where were my students' voices? I started to seek them out. "Who inspires you?" I asked workshop participants, and then added works by those writers to the living archive, too.

Today, I devote an entire course—The Inspiration Lab—to studying my students' artistic mentors. The living archive does not exist until they make it. In this radical take on the anthology, every workshop participant contributes to our course of study, selecting one art object to share: audio, image, text, or something in between. What I find remarkable is that the majority of participants instinctively select works by contemporary writers of color. We discuss their selections in terms of craft and then create art objects in response, the goal being to broaden our imaginations to access inspiration from everything, everywhere, regardless of the confines of personal aesthetic. In the process, we achieve a truly democratic classroom—a Marxist, Freirian, liberatory classroom.

Conversation as Context

A perk to reading contemporary writers is that they're not dead. Likely they're sitting around checking and rechecking their e-mail as a means to procrastinate from writing, so if you reach out to them with a request for a quick Skype chat, they're bound to respond promptly. When approached respectfully, they'll often say yes, because no matter what the success level, writers understand the value of mentorship in an otherwise isolated craft.

To supplement an author's ideas with an author's physical body has power. It humanizes the work. For example, just as a white stranger imposes meaning on a Black body, so, too, do white workshop participants impose meaning on work by writers of color. Both elicit fear, defensiveness, or confusion: this is not "normal." And so, they judge: this is unrelatable. Distance is integral to this judgement, for it reinforces the Other as foreign, inferior.

In her essay "Unsilencing the Writer's Workshop," author Beth Nguyen remembers workshopping a piece with her MFA cohort in which characters were on their way to dim sum:

In the workshop, people wanted to know what dim sum was. They couldn't ask me directly because it was workshop; the writer was supposed to stay silent and take notes. They spent some time talking about how dim sum must be something Asian but it was confusing and it made the whole piece confusing—they were distracted, you see, by not knowing what dim sum was. Of course the whole time I was thinking, really, you don't know what dim sum is? Also, why didn't you find out before workshop? . . . In this workshop format, the idea of what constituted basic knowledge did not include dim sum. They, the rest of the people in the workshop, decided what constituted basic knowledge. And yes, they were white. The group's knowledge *was* knowledge. I was the outsider, the strange Asian who needed to adapt my work to what they understood.[12]

A white workshop participant can choose to disengage with the ideas of a writer of color ("I didn't get it") without ever having to exercise the self-control to suspend judgement and reframe the context: this text doesn't serve my notion of normalcy (aka the white narrative Toni Morrison talks about which we can read as white supremacy), but I will challenge myself to listen. White workshop leaders tend to reinforce white students' disengagement as valid critique, for they constitute the "general readership" to which all writing allegedly aims to appeal. Compound this disengagement with enforced silence—writers aren't allowed to speak during workshop—and the equation is complete: judgement plus distance equals dehumanization.

How do we bring the body back into the work?

Step one is for workshop participants to write by hand.

Step two is for workshop participants to stand and read their work aloud so that we're forced to see them, fully embodied in front of us. We're forced to hear the words as shaped by their mouths, by their cadence.

Step three is for workshop participants to contextualize their own writing process and the writing of others by reading it with an awareness of the author's body and lived experience.

Step four is for workshop participants to suppress their immediate judgement of "good" or "bad" as irrelevant, and instead listen to the author's insights about their artistic process and project goals.

Step five is for workshop participants to respond to the author's questions about their own work with specific, grounded, craft-based feedback.

There's no electing out. We address the author by name. We quote the author's lines back to them. We ask for permission to express our opinions, and accept a response of "no" should the author want to move on. We do this so that our workshop participants decenter themselves as authorities on their peer's art. This requires more intensive action from our white students. They are not the norm by which we judge competence, clarity, and quality. Instead, they are collaborators in community, helping a fellow author to fulfill their artistic vision, the product of which may or may not be intended for them.

By bringing the body into the work, we train our workshop participants to not only humanize one another but also to decenter themselves. We demand dignity for everyone. Instead of an ignorant "I didn't get it," participants seek out understanding, posing questions about authorial intention and thematic context. As a result, participants engage in their own education.

But how to extend this practice to assigned readings, disembodied on the page or screen? We force these authors, too, into silence, while workshop participants pronounce judgement on the texts in class discussion. I remember classmates who threw books on the floor, declared them "garbage," a "total waste of time." Works by writers of color were prone to this sort of scathing critique. They were too confusing, inaccessible, self-indulgent, tedious, simplistic, or off-putting. Workshop discussion was less about what the texts offered to teach us and more about what we could teach the authors—primarily, how to write "right." To allow our workshop participants to judge reading assignments in this manner sets a dangerous precedent for free rein in future workshop. My own professors seemed bemused at students' strong responses, or worse, energized by it, playing devil's advocate in the author's defense. Inevitably, the professor would nod toward the token person of color in the room for confirmation on context: "Is that how you see it, Felicia?"

What if published authors were allowed to speak for themselves?

I advocate supplementing assigned readings by contemporary writers with short in-class interviews, as many as you're able to schedule per semester. Maybe these interviews occur online via Skype, maybe they occur in person (should the author happen to be on book tour or live in the area). Back when I was a teaching assistant, I'd pool what few resources I had, inviting fellow graduate students into my classroom every Friday for pizza, Coke, and conversation. (I should note here that, as a matter of principle, I always aim to pay writers for their time, be it in cash, gift card, or a decent spread of food. Often they'll visit for free, of course, but the gesture demonstrates respect.) No matter the caliber of professional writer, the shift in energy and perspective that a guest brings into the room is invaluable.

Rather than ingest an author's writing and regurgitate judgement, then, my workshop participants read assignments with awareness that a human being wrote these words, a person with backstory and body. As such, they prepare questions about craft (What was your strategy here, in stanza six, with those run-on sentences that got me so emotional?), context (Can you tell me more about the history behind this ceremony that you touch on in your essay?) and culture (What's your take on today's publishing industry?). They type and print a list of questions for the author, as opposed to the after-the-fact traditional letter telling them about the inherent value of their work.

Essential to the success of these interviews is training workshop participants in how to ask good questions. Understanding the art of the question is an invaluable, lifelong skill for any writer, and yet too often workshop leaders cross their fingers in hopes that students will show up, much less speak up, at readings. Together, my workshop participants study how to differentiate between closed and open-ended questions, how to formulate action-oriented questions, how to harness specificity to invoke richer responses, and how to fold in follow-up questions so as to not overwhelm the interviewee. I go so far as to provide our interview subject with a list of the students' questions so that they may identify a subject of personal interest: Jessie, I see here that you're curious about the sister character. Thus, raising the stakes, workshop participants are accountable for the success of the interview. The quality of the resultant questions enhances.

When we can't engage the author in person, students and I collect online interviews, blog posts, biographical data, and a photo to supplement the assigned reading. In this small way, workshop participants are still able to access the writer's voice. "What would we ask the author if we could?" I wonder aloud, and students practice posing questions.

Engaging the author is enough to restore their humanity. It dispels distance. It makes the foreign familiar by personalizing the words on the page. It invokes curiosity. It decenters students as authority, reconditioning their responses from critique to craft. It invites them to commune as writers, and as such, to claim the identity of author. After each interview, I exit the room not knowing if my workshop participants liked or disliked the work, and that's exactly as it should be. Instead, we close class on insights and strategies we've gleaned that we'd like to apply to our own work moving forward.

Restoring Literary Integrity

In this chapter, I spoke of completing the canon, as opposed to outright rejecting, replacing, or deconstructing the canon. I argued that canonical Western literature offers invaluable insight into imperialist, white supremacist ideology—ideology that is inherently dependent on and in reaction to people of color. To substitute one canon for another is to deny the opportunity to study these texts as multidimensional narratives: craft-rich poetry, prose, and plays, yes, but also strategic rhetoric for the preservation of whiteness as normal, neutral, and central (and, respectively, "nonwhiteness" as abnormal, marked, and marginalized).

The responsibility is ours, as workshop leaders, to critically engage the specter of Otherness that haunts these pages, for to deny its presence is to perpetuate an incomplete reading of the texts. We might choose to pair a "classic" canonical text in conversation with a historical or contemporary text by a writer of color. This side-by-side study acknowledges a cultural call and response; both are political texts in need of unpacking.

In *Playing in the Dark: Whiteness and the Literary Imagination* Toni Morrison writes:

> I do not want to alter one hierarchy in order to institute another.
> . . . More interesting is what makes intellectual domination possi-
> ble; how knowledge is transformed from invasion and conquest to
> revelation and choice; what ignites and informs the literary imagi-
> nation, and what forces help establish the parameters of criticism.[13]

This is the real work. Anti-racist workshop leaders, we must expose institutionalized literacy as a politics of domination. We give it a name: white supremacy. We speak that name aloud and study how it operates, from canon to curriculum to publishing industry to literary criticism. In doing so, we are able to imagine, initiate, and implement alternative choices for change in our own creative writing workshops. These choices for change are the sixth step to completing the canon, one classroom at a time.

For, realistically, there's no "instituting" one hierarchy in place of another. That shit's fixed. Even when I present my students with a living archive of young, contemporary writers of color, we instinctively reference the texts in response to white, male, Western authors. How could we not? The indoctrination runs deep, and I hate it, I hate it, I do, Ana Castillo. It's our job, then, to correct art's politics by speaking it into existence, over and over and over again: You exist—we do; they cannot erase us.

CHAPTER FIVE

Owning the Language of Craft

Negotiating Our Belonging

As a working class, first-generation undergraduate student, I had a nontraditional trajectory. Like so many young people of color, I had to figure things out on my own as I went along. There was financial aid, that labyrinthine blockade between college—"Where you belong!" my high school teachers chorused—and my broke ass. To belong meant convincing an anonymous authority that I was doubly deserving: both smart enough, and poor enough, for their institution's charity. FAFSA alone was proof that I was wrong for college, too illiterate to decode the required documentation. Perhaps if I were from a different race or social class, I'd have a name for it: unfair. To do more because I had less felt wrong. Pages upon pages of baffling financial lexicon, in addition to supplementary merit, minority, and need-based scholarship application essays, made applying to college a part-time job for this eighteen-year-old. Luckily, unfair was beyond my frame of reference; shit was just hard.

I remember that spring of my senior year of high school, when so many of my classmates waved their acceptance letters like flags. Without an accompanying financial aid award, the welcome packets in my own mailbox meant nothing. To gain admission did not imply a right of entry.

What psychological trauma: pinned in place by a poverty I must prove, uncertain if I was worthy of advancing my education another year forward. Because I had to reapply for aid every fall semester, hand outstretched, waiting, wondering, the stress of not knowing was constant. Which is why, when I sought to transfer from Wellesley College, I considered Colorado College, which offered a fixed, four-year financial aid plan, among my list of potential schools. No more hours wasted tearful in the Student Aid Office, arguing over a misapplied grant or an unfeasible gap in award money. What a relief that must be, I thought, to just be a student.

Again, spring arrived, and with it, congratulatory invitations to transfer into this or that school. Colorado College awarded me admission, plus an academic scholarship that included tuition, room and board, a complimentary laptop, funding for textbooks, and a special roster of pre-orientation, credit-bearing classes.

You are exceptional, the letter said.

You are accomplished, the letter said.

You are impressive, the letter said, and I was duly impressed: How could any other school compare?

I remember crying, reading that letter. For the first time, someone saw me, saw my years of struggle and said you, Felicia Rose, deserve better. That summer, I packed my clothes and shoes into garbage bags and drove six hours up I-25 from Albuquerque to Colorado Springs. According to my letter, I was to unload my belongings in the dorm and then join a cohort of scholarship fellows for a welcome dinner.

When I pulled into the parking lot, I was struck by how crowded it was. Parents, siblings, students huddled left and right, unloading vehicles in their Sunday best. "Whoa," I thought. "How many scholarship fellows are there, exactly?" Suspended in the cab of my Wrangler, I reread my acceptance letter: Exceptional, accomplished, impressive. When I surveyed the parking lot again, that's when I saw it, felt it, a deep-down defeat that made the air thick, my limbs thick.

Every one of us was brown.

I'm not proud of my response in that moment. In retrospect, I can appreciate an administrative effort to pointedly recruit students of color, to celebrate us as commendable and gift us with the financial resources to succeed. But back then, I felt duped. The admissions committee hadn't seen me, not really. They'd seen a racial demographic that needed bolstering, and my brown body served that purpose. Not one word of my acceptance letter indicated race as criteria for my prized academic scholarship. Had I known the real deal, I could have chosen to accept this racialized distinction as opposed to it being imposed upon me. Years later I would go on to accept an undergraduate McNair Fellowship, then a Graduate Dean's Fellowship, and finally a post-graduate Riley Scholar Fellowship. As it was, Colorado College cheated me out of an opportunity to make an informed decision about my body, my education, and my future.

Sitting in my Jeep, I remember how grateful I was that I'd driven up alone, that this shame was private. Shame because I wasn't exceptional enough, without race factoring in. Isn't that what my white friends used to argue? In an era of besieged affirmative action policies, the fact that I earned preferential points for race, or dare say satisfied a quota, marked me as a threat, another dark-skinned invader who stole hard-earned opportunities from my innocent, white peers. I remember howling at my white friends' claims of reverse racism, wild with indignation. Ironic that I clung to my stellar GPA and test scores as proof of admittance—exceptional, accomplished, impressive—only to be reduced to a PR makeover for a liberal white college. To trust in the autonomy of one's own accomplishments, that's a privilege only white people get to enjoy.

Eventually I got out of the car. It helped that I didn't have air conditioning, otherwise I might have turned around and driven back home. The truth was that I'd already declined acceptance at the other schools to which I'd applied. Where would that road home lead? Instead I feigned altitude sickness, sat out dinner, and slept, anticipating a refreshed perspective the next day.

My first special, pre-orientation, credit-bearing class was English. I joined my cohort of thirteen—what I later learned to be the entire first-year, incoming class of color—and took a seat. My knee jiggled, my pen tapped. Despite everything, I couldn't contain my excitement to be back in a college classroom.

Our professor was a red-faced white man in a guayabera. He introduced himself, then talked about his dedication to the program, how thanks to the program "the college hasn't lost a single minority student yet." I gathered that my prized academic scholarship was a diversity retention program called Bridge.

"Why Bridge?" I asked.

"The program will help you get a feel for college. It's a leg up, so to speak, so that when real classes start, you'll feel better prepared. Like here, in English, we'll hone our reading and writing skills so that you won't feel so left behind when the other students show up."

Meaning, when the majority of the white students show up.

My prized academic scholarship was a prerequisite of remedial coursework to "bridge" me—exceptional, accomplished, impressive—with my white peers. And, thus, my first lesson as a Colorado College student: my accolades were not fixed markers as I'd once presumed; they bent to white power, which decided for itself what I was capable of, congratulating me on my intelligence while assuming my ignorance. I did not own the language of my narrative.

I excused myself from class to use the restroom, and then walked back to the dorm. A group of white athletes had arrived on campus, their laughter secure in the summer air. I didn't want them to see me, so I ran, the freshly mowed grass wet on my legs. I packed my clothes and shoes back into wrinkled black garbage bags. On the desk, I left a letter stating that while I was grateful for the opportunity, I'd decided to disenroll in Colorado College.

It wasn't until I climbed back into my Jeep that I came undone. I mourned, screaming and sobbing into the steering wheel. What the fuck was I doing, walking away from all this money? Because of what? Ego? Wasn't it enough that I knew who I was, what I was capable of, even if it meant accommodating the school's provision of my inferiority?

Was this the price of my pride?

I was too young, then, to think it over, to talk it through with a college representative, to hear out the greater mission of Bridge. I started the engine, and that was that.

I'm still living with the consequences of that was that, including $25,000 in unpaid student loans. Here I thought I was preserving my dignity by being anonymous rather than exceptional, by paying thousands of dollars in tuition fees elsewhere rather than bartering my brownness. A high price to pay for the essential knowledge that all academic spaces are white spaces, all academic knowledge white knowledge, upon which I trespassed at my own physical, emotional, and psychological risk. Did it matter where I enrolled? My acceptance letters did not, would not ever, mean real acceptance. My history, my culture, my narrative, were all interpreted through white bias and then explained back to me. If I was to learn anything in college, I had to forgo control over what I thought I knew and assimilate to white supremacy. I had to figure it out on my own, unpacking knowledge deliberately curated for white, middle-class students by white, middle-class professors.

Memoirist Austin Channing Brown recounts the unpacking she did while in school:

> I had been responsible for decoding teachers' references to white middle-class experiences. *It's like when you're sailing . . .* or *You know how when you're skiing, you have to . . .* My white teachers had an unspoken commitment to the belief that we are all the same, a default setting that masked for them how often white culture bled into the curriculum. For example, when teachers wanted to drive home the point that we should do something daily, they often likened it to how you wash your hair every morning. It never occurred to them that none of the Black girls in the class did this. Knowing it was true for white people, and having gotten used to white teachers' assumption of universality, we would all nod our heads and move on. Who had time to teach the teacher?[1]

To no longer own the language of our narratives means students of color are tasked with what Brown calls "decoding," translating white universality into multicultural reality. Once again, we're asked to do more because we have less. Taking notes during lecture becomes a multistep analysis:

» What did the professor and/or the text say, exactly?

» To whom was this information tailored, and why?

» What else was communicated, either through omission or nonverbal body language?

» Can I separate my emotional response to what was communicated in order to access the required information?

» If not, am I able and/or willing to articulate my offense to the professor, risking potential emotional, psychological, or academic injury?

» Finally, how can I adapt this information to best serve my individual learning?

Talk about critical thinking! Rather than passively receive information, students of color engage in observation, analysis, interpretation, evaluation, and decision-making, all as a matter of recourse to access an education while protecting our sanity. We may not recognize it as such, but we learn how to decode instinctually so as to reject the academy's colonization of our consciousness. Instead, we negotiate our belonging in a white supremacist capitalist patriarchy (otherwise known as college). To choose otherwise is to find ourselves cast out and in debt.

Imagine if every one of our students engaged these critical thinking skills. Imagine if every one of them augmented their individual narratives (What does this mean to me?) with academic knowledge construction (What does this mean to us?). I argue that it's possible for creative writing students to own the language of craft so that no one needs a leg up, because everyone is on equal footing.

Students of color are our own damn bridge. We don't need white savior professors to hold our hand across gaping racial and socioeconomic disparities lest they lose a minority. What we need is for professors to concede our dignity, to value our intelligence, and to dismantle their own biased assumptions in the classroom—assumptions that deepen the very gaps they claim to mend. We need for professors to then go on and help white students do the same.

The traditional workshop model is rife with assumed knowledge. We throw around vague vocabulary as though it were common know-how: render this scene; raise the stakes; identify the take away. It's time to make these abstract ideas concrete. This chapter demands that all workshop participants have equal access to the language of craft. Unpacking multiple interpretations of craft enriches multicultural learning, primes students in how to read as writers, and empowers them to own the terms in workshop.

Craft as Cultural Code

When I facilitate trainings on the anti-racist workshop model, dedicated educators often ask, "Why allow workshop participants to guess at craft when I have valuable insights to offer? If the point is to make critical concepts concrete, shouldn't I be the one defining the terms?" While I agree (indeed, you're an elder with experience and know-how to share), I contend that you are but one voice among many. Your valuable insights spring not from immoveable truth, but from biased perspective; your body, culture, class, and privilege influence your knowledge construction. You have your way, but it is far from the only way. This is true no matter where you published or under whom you mentored.

Rather than require students of color to acclimate to your perspective (here's where white universality undermines sincere attempts to educate participants), an anti-racist writing workshop advocates that educators listen to and incorporate their students' perspectives. By engaging students in the definition process, you confirm that knowledge construction is fluid—that there are multiple interpretations of the "right" way to write—while simultaneously empowering students to claim ownership of their artistic community. Effectively, you're making room for what bell hooks calls "cultural codes."

In *Teaching to Transgress*, hooks writes:

> As I worked to create teaching strategies that would make a space for multicultural learning, I found it necessary to recognize . . . different "cultural codes." To teach effectively a diverse student body, I have to learn these codes. And so do students. This act alone transforms the classroom. Professor and students have to learn to accept different ways of knowing, new epistemologies, in the multicultural setting.[2]

Here hooks rejects a top-down educational model, inquiring into students as individuals: Who are you, and where do you come from? How does your identity influence your learning style? Now, how can we incorporate elements from your distinct perspective into our classroom culture so as to resist assumed knowledge and activate your education? The responsibility for this communal knowledge construction rests not only on the professor, but on students as well. As opposed to people of color preparing for when the other students show up, here the groundwork is shared: everyone must listen, everyone must learn.

This is what dignity looks like in action. Humility, too.

What if you said to students, "Teach me, please," even if you're sure you know the answers, neatly summarized in your PowerPoint lecture? What if you encouraged them to speak from their experience, then validated their viewpoint as beneficial to the classroom community?

With a shift in perspective, an "uncooperative student" (disengaged, inarticulate, slow to learn) becomes a silenced student, who encouraged by validation begins to use their voice. A "burdensome student" (aggressive, confrontational, disruptive) becomes a starved student, who nourished by the cultural content they were invited to bring into the room, becomes a peer-teacher. Let's relinquish control over our students' narratives and allow for different ways of being, knowing.

David Mura reveals that recognizing different cultural codes is second nature in writing workshops designed by and designated for people of color, such as at VONA, the Voices of Our Nations Arts Foundation:

> Students speak of feeling a sense of safety and sanity at VONA. What so many realize—and what I myself have also realized—is that it is the white world which makes us feel crazy and which acts towards us in insane ways. In a world where the epistemology and ontology of Whiteness is not the dominant mode, we feel safer, saner. We can critique each other's work because we understand the literary, theoretical, cultural, historical and political background of that work. Just as importantly, we know and understand the experiences and communities from which that work derives. For most white writing teachers to provide such education, they must first acknowledge their ignorance, how little they actually know about our world. But that would require . . . a dismantling of ego that would go far beyond any reading list or literary instruction I could provide.[3]

To dismantle the ego—dominance, control, and the insistence of white universality—is to actively pursue an anti-racist writing workshop. First, we must admit to not knowing (Teach, me, please). Then, we must listen, and insist that students listen, too. As a writing community, we must hold one another accountable to a multiplicity of perspectives grounded in diverse historical and cultural contexts. We do this out of respect, generosity, and humility. We do this to become better people, better teachers, and better writers. The point is to radically reorient workshop away from a white supremacist arena of individualism and rivalry into a supportive, multicultural collective of writers with voice.

People of color are already doing this work among ourselves. It's time we felt safe, and sane, in workshops with white professors and peers.

It is not merely a small gesture; inviting students to collectively define craft concepts—concepts that will guide their reading of one another's texts, inform their workshop critique, and direct their self-evaluations—is, in practice, an unprecedented act of acceptance: they belong, for real. Engage them as individuals, exercise their critical thinking skills, and collaborate on communal knowledge construction. In doing so, we ensure that every workshop is reflective of its participants, as opposed to our personal perspectives.

Owning the Terms

It's so satisfying to truly understand what someone else means when they speak about your work. Many of my students admit that they never really listened to one another in past workshops because they were too preoccupied defending their craft choices, for your interpretation of "good" and my interpretation of "good" deviated so radically. Here's a chance for real creative community, the sort that works toward a collective goal without shutting anyone out.

It all starts with reading.

I joke with participants that reading an assigned text in workshop triggers the anxious English student in all of us. We process the text for information—evidence to support our opinion of liking or not liking the piece, condemning it as "good" or "bad"—then skim it again during class for something smart-sounding to say (I remember there being a passage that was soooo Freudian—wait, just let me find it . . . I know it's in here somewhere . . .). It's no wonder so many English students go on to law school. We're experts at defending our argument. But unlike English class, the creative writing student does not communicate in thesis-driven essays.

Rather than read to support a claim, I encourage my workshop participants to *feel* their way through a text. When they hit upon an embodied response—a bark of a laugh, a sigh, a wandering mind—it's up to them to interrogate why. What was it, exactly, that evoked the response? I want them to put the text up on blocks, so to speak, and deconstruct its insides: How does this thing function as a work of art?

We read for craft.

An emphasis on craft teaches workshop participants how to read as writers rather than future defense attorneys. They must side-step their egos, let go of liking or not liking a text, to better listen and learn. What is the text teaching them about rhythm, imagery, narrative structure? As writers we are responsible for scavenging our own inspiration. We must pursue craft daily, in everything from the back of the cereal box to the box office release. If we waited to study only that which we liked, our artistic production would stagnate. With adequate practice, we can train our brains to identify craft on command, irrespective of opinion. This doesn't mean we always aim to attempt the technique—sometimes the lesson is in what to avoid on the page—it just means that we're accumulating tools for our toolboxes.

Using the assembled living archive, I organize my assigned texts into four craft categories: voice, imagery, characterization, and arrangement (what students call "flow"). I chose these particular categories after reflecting on my students' organic learning trajectory in workshop. First, we tackle the common conflation of the individual voice and the authorial voice (I was depressed when I wrote this, so the voice is totally emo). By distancing the writer from the writing, students learn to craft a compelling narrative persona tailored to each project. We then go on to make concrete the creative writing cliché, "Show, don't tell," breaking down figurative language into a balanced portrait of abstract comparison and sensory detail. Next, we aim to animate our text via characterization, layering in scene, setting, and dialogue. And finally, there's arrangement, an attempt to break free from a chronological story straightjacket. Rather than a strict allegiance to plot, we explore what our work is really about, structuring our narratives to best showcase our themes.

Obviously, these categories are interchangeable based on the workshop leader's goals. The texts within each category are inter-changeable as well, as any one text exhibits multiple, simultaneous craft elements at play. I like to select texts according to their bold-ness. Where is the author taking the most risk, in terms of voice, imagery, characterization, or arrangement? Maybe that risk pays off, maybe it doesn't, but I want to challenge my workshop participants to appreciate the author's audacity to experiment in the hopes that when it comes time for workshop, they'll feel free to experiment, too.

Students choose one or more texts from the assigned category (often I encourage them to self-select their nightly reading, other times I guide them toward readings I think speak to their individual aesthetic). The prompt is simple: Study the text(s), and then answer the question, "What is voice?" in your writer's notebook. When we reconvene for class discussion, we all know exactly what we're going to talk about (and yes, everyone is required to talk). There's no one person dominating the discussion, there's no scrambling to sound smart, there's no proving a point; all students are equally vulnerable in positing a definition. True, students reference different source material, and this makes some educators uncomfortable, but I find that it allows opportunity for students to exercise summation, a skill they'll later apply to their own work come workshop.

"So, what is voice?" I'll lead, standing in front of the white board, marker in hand. Students take exactly as long as they need to brainstorm definitions—sometimes a swift fifteen minutes, sometimes the entire class period. Occasionally I'll volunteer my own ideas if I feel that the group has overlooked something, but never with the expectation that my interpretation is the only right interpretation. After much discussion, students agree on a succinct definition of the craft element that they will then uphold in their own work. In effect, they're co-creating a lexicon for workshop critique.

Depending on the experience level of the group, I might assign students follow-up "milestone" exercises in which they demonstrate the craft element in action. They begin with a short scene that exhibits voice, then move on to write a scene that exhibits both voice and imagery, and so on and so forth until they juggle all four craft elements simultaneously. "I never knew writing involved so much choice!" students often tell me, and I smile, pleased that they are reading their own work as writers.

When it's time for formal workshop, participants are practiced at speaking in craft and prepared to assess their own writing in those same terms. In fact, every participant up for workshop artic-ulates three craft-based questions to guide our discussion of their work. The group responds, question by question, from a place of communal knowledge. As a collective, we appreciate one another's divergent aesthetics, but still hold one another accountable to a foundation in craft.

My goal is to empower students with the language of their trade so that they may revisit the page with renewed insight. As one young woman wrote in her end-of-semester reflection, "I'd never tried to explain point of view, tone of voice. No one had ever asked. Now I have direction, control, purpose."

A Note on Reading for Craft over Content

During a recent speech, my husband (a brilliant educator) said that we cop out when we don't teach how identity politics influence narrative content. He went on to explain that a blind fixation on craft "is a cover for avoiding issues of marginalization and politics of narrative." I know he wasn't calling me out, specifically, but I admit to feeling shamed, sitting there in the audience as every-one nodded their heads in agreement. Was I not doing enough to bridge the divide between craft and content? Could I better honor my students' stories?

As it stands, I leave it up to the author to address the content of their narrative. Whether it be digital or in-person dialogues with published guests, supplementary interviews that accompany as-signed readings, or among ourselves during workshop critique, I task participants with reading, listening, reflecting, and asking questions about one another's work in order to educate themselves about cul-tural disparities. I want to foster an inclusive learning community of inquisitive and informed workshop participants, but I don't believe that it's my place to speak on behalf of another author.

I'll be the first to admit that I have a lot to learn, moving for-ward. How do I integrate more direct instruction on content, I won-dered, while still advancing an anti-racist workshop?

Lord knows I'm set on what I don't want to have happen. In the traditional writing workshop, participants study white authors to learn the art of writing—that is, they absorb and then imitate craft concepts as an initial step toward honing their skills on the page. Workshop leaders might lecture on a particularly challenging story structure or narrative technique, but the predominant assumption of white universality means that content—a play by play of plot points—is not of primary concern, aside from the occasional pop quiz. Unless, of course, workshop leaders teach Baldwin, who is treated as a placeholder for Diversity. Then content is king, for we must endeavor to navigate this foreign world, unfurling plot points to discover the meaning of the text. We'll need Baldwin's biography as context, as well as a nonfiction primer on the historical period in question. We'll need a self-conscious discussion about race so as to get at Baldwin's deeper purpose for writing the text. It's disappointing, of course, when the occasional white student doesn't get it, can't relate, or feels attacked, but the point is exposure, right? What a tired, lazy, self-congratulatory approach.

Workshop leaders' treatment of the text is rooted in sociology; artfulness comes second, if at all. But if there's no such thing as neutrality—if all art is political art—then why do identity politics only surface when reading writers of color? Why aren't workshop leaders scrutinizing authorial race and racialized content when it comes to white writers and their (presumably) white characters (for a lack of racial tagging automatically translates to "normal," or white, right)? Why aren't workshop leaders scrutinizing white writers' often egregious mishandling of characters of color? Is whiteness so protected as to achieve invisibility?

I once had a creative nonfiction professor who "diversified" his syllabus by featuring three or four white authors who embedded themselves in communities of color so as to capture their stories. The artfulness of the selections was evident enough—Anne Fadiman's *The Spirit Catches You and You Fall Down* and Dave Egger's *What Is the What* come to mind—and yet I couldn't get past the fact that we never once formally confronted the problematic politics of these ethnographic reconstructions. You better believe I brought it up in class discussion, only to get shot down by my white peers, who reassured me that they thought it was fine. A few students went so far as to e-mail the professor, attesting that there was nothing wrong with his reading list, that it was me who was making a big deal out of nothing. I know this because the professor shared it with me one day after class, perhaps as evidence in his defense, perhaps to ostracize me into silence. I dared to comment on content—the deeper purpose behind white writers' claiming ownership over the narratives of people of color—only to receive dismissal from my professor and peers. Now, when we went on to read our only author of color—dead, of course—in this case Zora Neale Hurston—the bells of Blackness rang loud, alarming the class that we were on unfamiliar ground.

Enough with this fumbling, lopsided consideration of content. Isolating writers of color as Other, necessitating exhaustive analysis lest white readers feel lost, is the equivalent of parading the exotic specimen at the fair. What's worse, by handholding students through POC texts so that the content feels safe, easy to understand, and relatable to a white "norm," traditional workshop leaders train their white students to do the same. I remember an hour-long workshop in which my peers fixated on how guilty my essay made them feel about their white privilege. They debated whether feeling bad was worth the read, among themselves for the entirety of my workshop time, since as a fly on the wall in a traditional workshop I was not entitled to intervene. I left workshop with no revision notes and a certainty that I'd bury this essay, because if white readers didn't like it, then no one would, right?

Too often, writers of color feel like we must accommodate white readers' bogus entitlement to our narrative. An assessment of our artfulness—the whole point of critique—is beyond the time constraints of workshop. Honing our skills on the page, then, is a matter of clarity first ("Will a white reader get it?") and craft second.

In sum, the traditional writing workshop reinforces the omnipotence of white readers and stunts writers of color. Forget all that.

So how, then, do I avoid the cop-out?

In *A Stranger's Journey: Race, Identity, and Narrative Craft in Writing*, David Mura argues that is our responsibility as workshop leaders to stop segregating literature—and consequently, our workshop participants' texts—into white and Other, familiar and foreign. If we are to engage in a literary analysis of identity politics alongside craft concepts, then we must apply that treatment to each and every work we encounter.

Mura aims "to broaden the essential elements of the writer's craft" to include issues of race and ethnicity, so as to end "the assumption of a monochromatic readership . . . in the white literary imagination."[4] He asks:

> Do whites lack a racial identity while only people of color possess one? Obviously, this notion is absurd. Is it people of color who gave themselves their racial identity? No, historically white people have done this. Is the identity and experience of people of color based solely on the practices of people of color? Again, the answer is no. Examining the fallacies invoked here leads to several revealing questions concerning race and literature. The first is, *If the very way white writers introduce their characters and the very way writers of color introduce their characters are racialized, how is it that any piece of American fiction, whether written by a white person or a person of color, escapes being racialized?* What would our literature look like if this rule were not the norm? How difficult is it for whites to identify themselves as white? And what exactly is the cause of this difficulty? When writers of color acknowledge their racial reality, what does this allow them to accomplish in their writing? Does the fact that most white writers don't do so indicate that these writers are simplifying or leaving out parts of their reality? How are these two different literary practices related to what we deem craft and artistic excellence?[5]

These questions, Mura argues, are central to the intellectual paradigm shifts happening all around us. *A Stranger's Journey* serves as a pivotal primer on how to teach twenty-first century literary analysis. To do so we must concede that racial identity politics influence narrative content, and as such, are crucial to craft.

This is hard work.

Are we, as anti-racist workshop leaders, prepared to teach real diversity—the kind that looks inward as well as outward, that investigates the history of colonialism, racism, sexism, classism, and white identity politics when applied to Baldwin as well as beloved white authors? As artist and activist Lilla Watson reminds us, "If you have come here to help me you are wasting your time, but if you have come because your liberation is bound up with mine, then let us work together."[6] Rather than exercising ownership over the narratives of people of color, as my professor and peers sought to, it is time for us to own up to, and break down, the politics of white narratives. Maybe this is the one and true "bridge," where we meet in the middle as opposed to crossing over.

CHAPTER SIX

Teaching Writers to Workshop

At the Crossroads

I remember the first time my body knew that a teacher was wrong. I was in third grade and best friends with a white girl named Franny. Mrs. Snyder-Bryant asked us to hang back from recess one day, presumably to mediate our morning-long bickering—over what, I haven't a clue. I remember the eerie quiet of the classroom, that hard plastic seat, how Mrs. Snyder-Bryant leaned forward when she said, "Felicia, dear, I think you're jealous of Franny." I remember studying her face: pale, set in a sad clown smile like she pitied poor me. My body responded immediately with, "That's some bullshit," but my mouth said, "Oh." And then later, after much coaxing, "I'm sorry, Franny. Will you forgive me?"

This memory surfaces a lot. Maybe it was the certitude with which I held my ground—internally, at least—unable to be swayed by Mrs. Snyder-Bryant's authority. For a good girl like me, it was rare not to contort my conviction to agree with the teacher. Over the years, as the mediations became more complex, this internal resistance faltered. I still registered my body's protest, but was quick to doubt myself. Maybe I was being too sensitive, too defensive, too irrational? Likely it was me who was wrong.

Mrs. Snyder-Bryant came to mind again while I was in graduate school at the University of Iowa. I'd nearly wrapped my core credit requirements, with one writing workshop left to complete. Just thinking about that last workshop made me want to run circles in the yard, crazed like a neglected dog. The anxiety was real; I couldn't do it, couldn't subject myself to the rage, the humiliation, one minute more. And so I petitioned the department chair to substitute a Studio Art workshop instead, seeing as my work was multimedia in scope. I made a mighty case for the switch, but I think the chair was fine to outsource me elsewhere.

Due to a recent flood, Studio Art lived in an old Menard's hardware store while the campus underwent repair. The impact of that cavernous space was awesome. Here was a colony of artists, islanded from the university and subject to their own rules. My Intermedia Art workshop taught me just how different this set was from my own.

"You're wrong," a blue-haired filmmaker informed us, her workshop professor and peers, after we invested a good half hour to discussing her short. Her art was abstract, lots of silence and masks and food smeared on bodies. I was way out of my element, so I sat back and observed the workshop, how impersonal the whole thing felt, like a collective shrug of shoulders. Students' feedback was predictably prescriptive (You need to change the opening; It'd be better if it ended here) but the artist, impervious, talked back point by point. "No," she'd say. "I like it the way it is." And so we'd move on without debate. Every now and then she'd nod at a suggestion, scribble it in her Moleskin and thank the contributor, but the majority of the workshop showcased her conviction. She knew her work. And we trusted that she knew her work. Unlike my usual writing workshops, Intermedia Art wasn't an arena of domination and control, in which participants competed to know best, filibustering their opinions at the expense of progress.

How did these students get so lucky, I wondered? Was it just a visual artist thing, to uphold one's internal conviction and claim the privilege to speak it aloud?

I went on to enroll in a book arts elective, whose students were so generous and encouraging with one another that it stunned me into silence, despite the fact that I was yet again allowed voice during workshop. Our room was lamp lit and radiator hot, a balm for Iowa's long winter. We'd gather around a wooden table stained with letterpress ink and ask question after question—"What inspired this project?" "How do you see it evolving?"—never judging the work as publication ready, but as an idea in progress. In all that back and forth, I found myself articulating aspects of my art that I hadn't had the time or space to consider during the drafting stage. Talking shop helped me to illuminate what I wanted in a revision. True, I left class guessing at others' opinion of my work, but with time, I caught on that my classmates weren't the point; here was opportunity to listen to and trust in myself.

"Fluff" was the response I got when I tried to convey the book arts workshop model to my fellow writers: "I don't want all that fluff. I want the truth." Why, I wondered, did we writers—so discerning about the complexities of the human condition on the page—forgo nuance in workshop critique? The work is either "good" or "bad." Be brutal. Rip into it. Is it insecurity that causes our perspective to narrow so, demanding dichotomy as truth?

Isolation had me convinced that critique meant only one thing, but that was far from true. It took me stepping out of the English Department and exposing myself to other arts programs to learn that varied, dynamic approaches to workshop existed elsewhere. I audited a performance writing workshop in which students crafted lyrics on the spot, then shared them aloud. One by one, their peers offered a "pop," quoting back a particular moment of heightened energy or innovation—a line, a rhyme, an image—in celebration of what was working in the piece. Imagine my surprise when class then moved on to a lecture segment. "That was it?" I thought. "A workshop consisting entirely of praise?" I was troubled by my own skepticism, so trained in a tradition of callousness and competition. My nonfiction cohort tended to roll their eyes if we began workshop with praise, the consensus being that we were wasting the author's time with forced flattery. It took me a couple of class sessions to witness how pops nurtured early work, bolstering participants' confidence and gifting them with leads to pursue in later drafts (previously discussed in chapter 3).

I went on to audit a photography workshop, then a playwriting workshop. I interviewed dancers and musicians about how they critiqued one another's art. Beyond how, I wanted to know why they workshopped the way that they did. Was there something inherent to that particular art form that necessitated a different approach? More to the point, what was it about writing, or writers, that cultivated the traditional workshop model? I myself had chosen to implement a different approach in my classroom, but that was purely a reactionary move against abusive, racist policies. I hadn't yet nailed down my pedagogy beyond "fuck you."

"You're wrong," I wanted to tell my creative writing professors. I felt it in my body, how our arts community could be productive and healthy and inclusive, if only we were open to change.

Unfortunately, so much of teaching is about inheritance, about reinforcing the way it's always been done. Many of us can't even articulate why we workshop the way that we do, beyond tradition serving as a rite of passage. Consider:

» Who were you when you first began writing?

» Who mentored you along your journey?

» Who failed you, criticized you, belittled the art as a waste of time?

» Who inspired you to write regardless?

Every one of us carries this creative inheritance into the classroom, through our choice of dress, demeanor, curriculum, and evaluative measures. Whether or not we're aware, creative heritage has present-day weight and substance. It's the same with cultural heritage. Where we're from (and how we "read") influences our relationship to and assumption of inherent rights, benefits, and advantages. As educators, this bias perpetuates our classroom policies.

In *Acts of Faith*, author and activist Eboo Patel describes his adolescent struggle to reconcile his American, Indian, and Islamic heritage as "standing at the crossroads of inheritance and discovery, trying to look both ways at once."[1] How could he learn from, love, and yet adapt these seemingly mutually exclusive identities to achieve balance? He asks: "How might I embrace the parts that are humanizing, change the parts that hurt and marginalize, make them my own?"[2] As twenty-first-century anti-racist workshop leaders, it is up to us to resist inheritance as default ("It's the way I was taught; it worked fine for me") and instead consider Patel's journey. What might we learn if we swiveled our heads at the crossroads, inviting discovery into our periphery? If the way it's always been done hurts and marginalizes a subset of our students, how might we adapt our habits to actively achieve plurality?

When I say this to fellow professors—that there's more than one way to workshop, that you don't have to fall back on inheritance—they often respond from fear. "Really? You think I could get away with it?" And then, after a pause, "Maybe I could start small, you know? Work up to the bigger stuff later on."

Some early career professors are afraid of getting into trouble for deviating from the norm.

Some mid-career professors are afraid they might score poorly on their tenure review if they start initiating change now.

Some late-career professors are afraid of the effort a curricular overhaul will entail.

Every one of them vocalizes fear that a break with inheritance will cause them to lose authority in the creative writing classroom.

I hear it again and again, this nervous insistence on preserving authority. And I get it. When I first started teaching in the college classroom, colleagues insisted that I invest in a professional wardrobe, the implication being that because I am a petite woman of color, my writing students would "walk all over me" if I presented informally. And so it was pencil skirts and collared shirts, a professorial costume meant to command authority. I was miserable in my Ann Taylor pastels, but I assumed that this particular brand of formality was fitting because it was what my white professors modeled throughout my undergraduate education.

"Never give in to a student," insisted these same colleagues, "or they'll take advantage of you." And so, I devised a similarly formal classroom persona, the sort that stared, bored, out of my office window until a student stopped crying. As I grew in confidence as a teacher, I ditched the wardrobe, ditched the ice queen act. I no longer feared that my students and I were adversaries, vying to win control of the classroom. Yet still, even today, some ten years later, I hear the old guard caution new hires to protect their authority, lest they lose face.

Is this what's at the heart of our creative inheritance, then? Power. Control. Domination. Maybe the solitary act of writing feeds the egoist in all of us. Surely, when it comes to the page, we're out for number one, susceptible to highs of narcissism and lows of neuroticism (that's where the fear sneaks in). But must this egocentric authority subvert workshop?

This chapter prompts us to interrogate our creative and cultural inheritance with the goal of discovering possibilities beyond the traditional writing workshop. Having traversed the arts landscape, I've witnessed firsthand how critique can evolve into a proactive art form. In my own classroom, participants check their egos and rally around one another, training in how to summarize their work, devise discussion questions, read in service of the author's agenda, articulate constructive questions, and moderate feedback. This student-centered model empowers participants to exercise kinship and own their workshop experience.

Every student deserves the opportunity to trust their creative impulse. Every student deserves the opportunity to exercise their own authentic voice. Every student deserves the opportunity to uphold their convictions. Anti-racist workshop leaders, it's time to relinquish our stronghold on being right, and admit that we can do better.

Taking Stock

Why do we workshop student writing? Is it to enact "real world" accountability on deadline? Is it to reinforce consistent, independent writing production? Is it to judge a student's talent against a pool of their peers? Maybe it's to enhance students' editing and analytical skills so that they may discover who they are as readers.

Most would answer that the purpose of the writing workshop is to develop aspiring writers, offering insight into one another's works in progress via a supportive arts community.

Sounds good, but is this what's really going down in our classrooms?

To develop aspiring writers, participants must write and share their work aloud as often as possible—preferably every day (see chapter 3)—so as to combat perfectionism, temper fear, curb the competitive impulse, and normalize risk. Yet the average workshop participant publicly shares their writing at best twice per semester, forgoing opportunities for failure and upping the pressure to get it right the first time. The way things are now, workshop serves as a litmus test. Participants either have what it takes, or they don't.

Paradoxically, this pressure gives rise to procrastination. Rather than present polished drafts in workshop, I remember writers from my MFA cohort who would share whatever it was they could jam out in time (or worse, recycle work that's proven "safe" in the past). Such writing spikes feelings of anxiety, self-loathing, or defensiveness. It wasn't uncommon for these students to drink alcohol before or cry after a workshop as a means of self-soothing. This is a lesson in resilience, not growth. For students of color especially, limited opportunities to exercise voice can rupture a burgeoning relationship to writing. All it takes is one bad, high-stakes workshop experience and suddenly writing's not really their thing. For MFA students, this rupture can be devastating.

To truly develop as writers, participants need ample opportunity to practice. How else can they measure their individual growth over time?

To offer insight into one another's works in progress, participants must cultivate artistic intuition. This takes time and effort. It's a skill students learn over the course of workshop. It's up to us to teach them how to pose questions about their own writing and the writing of others, and—of equal importance—how to listen to themselves and others with respect and humility.

The average workshop participant undergoes zero training in how to offer critique. Instead, they wield bias as weapon, mistaking ego for objectivity. Rather than insight, participants besiege authors with judgement and opinion. How many ghosts of workshops past haunt the psyches of developing writers (This is beyond fixing; I just don't see the point of your piece; Maybe put this away in a drawer somewhere)?

Deferring our personal aesthetic preferences to those of the author necessitates curiosity, sensitivity, and a keen awareness of one's own positionality. If we aspire for our students to offer insight into one another's work, then we need to incorporate such skills building into our workshop curriculum.

To foster a supportive arts community, participants must exercise joint ownership of the writing workshop. This goes beyond sharing physical space. Real community is collective rather than individualistic, active rather than passive, centered on trust rather than transaction. Do your students collaborate on the workshop's rules and rituals? Do they collectively develop a workshop vocabulary? Are they empowered to speak during workshop? Do they engage in post-workshop reflections so as to routinely strengthen the practicum? Most importantly, do they know one another, trust one another?

I can't tell you how many professors flaunt a supportive arts community, and yet students don't even know one another's names! While this may read as a small detail, it is acutely important that our students of color have names, bodies, weight, and substance so as to combat racial bias and invisibility. Every student and instructor in the room must belong. To promote such kinship, anti-racist workshop leaders must humanize our approach, devoting time and attention to the people in the class over a rote adherence to the day's agenda.

Before you move forward in this book, I encourage you to take stock of your present-day practices. Ask yourself:

» Why do I workshop?

» How does my workshop philosophy differ from my classroom reality?

» How do my workshop rituals resume traditions from my creative inheritance (the manner in which you were taught)?

» How do my workshop rituals impose attributes from my cultural inheritance (your personal biases, values, and assumptions)?

» What opportunities do I have to extend beyond my inheritance, welcoming discovery and initiating change in my curriculum?

» Who might this change better serve, and why?

It is up to you to achieve balance between the way it's always been done and the way it could be. Embrace risk.

The remainder of this chapter outlines my personal negotiation of inheritance and discovery in the creative writing classroom, but it's just a blueprint. Take what works for you, adapt it, grow it. We aim to develop aspiring writers, yes, but let's not forget that we aim to develop as workshop leaders, too.

My Foundation:
The Liz Lerman Critical Response Process

It was my husband who first introduced me to Liz Lerman. He'd recently participated in a two-day theater workshop that employed her methodology and was curious about my take on it. To this day, I credit Liz Lerman as a pivotal influence on my creative writing pedagogy. Here was someone who articulated what I'd felt for years—that something was wrong—but took it a step further, creating tangible change by evolving a system of peer response that felt right. It didn't faze me in the least that she came from the world of dance. My fieldwork outside of English had taught me to embrace alternative approaches from a variety of arts programs.

"Though critique had been a familiar companion from my earliest days as a child in dance class," reflects Lerman, "I was well established in my career as a choreographer before I finally acknowledged how uncomfortable I was about most aspects of criticism." She continues:

> I began to question the basic premises underlying my teaching of dance composition because I was troubled about the nature of my response to the work being created by my students. I had plenty to say. That wasn't the problem. But I kept wondering why I was saying it: Was I truly helping my students find their individual voices or was I just trying to create clones of me? Moreover, when I was at the receiving end of criticism—whether positive or negative—I had a sense that there was a supposedly mature way to hear comments of others . . . To respond in this "mature" way to criticism meant quietly taking it, rather than attempting to engage in a dialogue, since to respond at all was somehow deemed a violation of an unspoken boundary.[3]

By daring to question the underlying values implicit in giving and receiving criticism, Lerman reveals how silence is a tool of the traditional workshop model to maintain domination and control. If our biased aesthetic preferences influence how we respond to others' work, then critique is a mere manifestation of our competitive impulse as artists (Validate me and my creative work by mirroring what I do). Whether consciously or subconsciously, we shun artists into self-imposed silence in order to prevent them from succeeding on their own terms, insisting instead that they judge their work according to our personal values and assumptions. For artists of color, workshop can function as a rite of erasure, tyrannizing self-expression into silence in order to reinstate and reproduce (white) creativity, (white) imagination, and (white) autonomy. Seen in this light, criticism becomes more about the individual egos of workshop participants than about the art being workshopped.

In attempt to democratize the process and "talk about work so that people could in fact have a dialogue and strengthen their own ability to solve the problems inherent in creative endeavors," Lerman invented an alternative, artist-centered workshop model.[4] She tested a prototype with the dancers in her company back in 1990. Over time, this model evolved into what is now the Critical Response Process, a four-step methodology inspiring specific, insightful, and constructive feedback.

I introduce Lerman's methodology about a quarter of the way through the semester, well in advance of our formal workshop. I require that students purchase the slim workshop manual, Liz Lerman's *Critical Response Process: A Method for Getting Useful Feedback on Anything You Make, From Dance to Dessert*, as ready reference. Then we read the text aloud in class and outline it on the board.

Step One: Participants Offer Statements of Meaning: "What was stimulating, surprising, evocative, memorable, touching, challenging, compelling, unique, delightful?"[5] After sharing their work, the artist prompts participants to provide statements of meaning. Note that participants refrain from "liking" an aspect of the artist's work, as such feedback is vague and unhelpful and tends to circle back to the responder ("I really like the mom character, because it reminds me of my friend's mom, who is so sweet. Like, this one time, she . . ."). Instead, Lerman challenges participants to expand their vocabularies in an effort to provide statements of meaning that are both specific and evidence-based ("Your opening paragraph was really challenging, in a good way. That onslaught of sensory detail disoriented me, but also compelled me to read more. I wanted to know what was happening. For example, here, when you write . . ."). Workshop members collectively witness the fact that the art has significance; there's value inherent to the work as is.

Step Two: Artist Poses Questions: "When the artist starts the dialogue, the opportunity for honesty increases."[6] In Step Two, the artist moderates a dialogue about their work, posing a series of craft-based questions that are neither too broad (What'd y'all think?) nor too narrow (Is that exclamation point too over the top?). The goal is for the artist to elicit pointed feedback on aspects of their work that matter most, taking into consideration where the draft is at in the development process. The ensuing discussion is free-flowing yet focused, candid yet respectful. The artist has the power to stop discussion and move on to another question once they feel like they've achieved an answer, or else follow up with additional questions in pursuit of a more satisfactory response. Step Two guarantees the artist feedback on their most pressing concerns, ensuring that workshop is never wasted.

Step Three: Respondents Pose Neutral Questions: "The Critical Response Process emphasizes the benefits of getting artists to think about their work in a fresh way, as opposed to telling them how to improve their work or asking them to defend it."[7] Neutral questions check participants' impulse to fix others' work by imposing their personal values of "good" and "bad" (You need to cut all this exposition and show rather than tell). Instead, participants remove themselves from the center of critique and inquire about the artist's primary intention (How would you categorize your voice in this essay?). As a result, workshop participants gain deeper insight into how to best aid the artist in achieving their vision (That's a great question, thanks for asking. I'm writing in the tradition of Richard Rodriguez, do you know him? I'm aiming for a political statement anchored in autobiographical essay, rather than a more traditional, narrative nonfiction approach). As is often the case, the question-answer exchange helps the artist think through aspects of their own work. They see for themselves what needs fixing.

Step Four: Participants Raise Permissioned Opinions: "Many of our reactions to work, which we may hold to be balanced, informed criticism, can also be viewed simply as subjective opinion."[8] Neutral questions help participants weigh the relevancy of their opinions. Should they still feel the need to offer prescriptive feedback on the artist's work, Step Four implements a protocol to preserve the artist's power. Participants name the topic of their opinion and then ask for permission to express themselves (I have an opinion about your title. Do you want to hear it?). The artist can defer the opinion

(Maybe later, if there's time), welcome it (Of course!) or politely decline, either because the topic is irrelevant to their goals, the topic is played out and they want to move on, or because they don't care to hear from that particular participant (No, but thank you). Step Four affords the artist opportunity to consciously pivot among ideas without feeling ambushed, which in turn increases their reception of the critique.

Once we outline Lerman's methodology and clarify questions, we go on to talk about how this workshop model differs from the traditional workshop model, and why.

Rarely do we afford students the opportunity to speak publicly about their past workshop experiences. I find that the discussion can get quite emotional, particularly for writers of color, queer writers, and working-class writers who've suffered emotional and psychological violence from toxic critique. On the other hand, one or two straight white students might dismiss the Lerman method as "soft," defending the traditional model as "more like real life." This is ideal timing to point out how our positionality influences our workshop experience and shapes our personal aesthetic preferences.

I dedicate one more class period to practicing the Lerman method as is, usually by workshopping a rough draft of something I've written. We analyze the strengths and weaknesses of my discussion questions (Step Two), then go on to devote a significant amount of time to Step Three, sidestepping opinion in favor of discovery. I find that this early exposure broadens students' tolerance toward an alternative workshop model and primes them to consider how to tailor the Lerman method to best serve their particular arts community.

Adapting the Methodology: The Artist Statement

As a foundational study in the way it could be, the *Critical Response Process* is a game changer. Still, I adapt the methodology in my own classroom to best serve creative writing students and further distance myself as workshop authority. Lerman delineates three specific workshop roles: facilitator (or workshop leader), artist, and responders. The artist moderates the workshop discussion, but it is the facilitator who guides the process along, intervening step-by-step to help the artist and responders more clearly articulate their ideas. This goes beyond checking students when they deviate from the process; it's our responsibility as workshop leaders to confront and challenge students' racist, sexist, classist, and homophobic behavior clearly, directly, and in the moment. Yet it's equally emboldening for the artist to shut that shit down. How many times do we as people of color want to say something, but we can't, or we don't, or we won't, out of fear?

With enough time and training, it's possible to empower artists to serve as both facilitator and moderator. When workshop is truly about the work, and not the egos of the participants or a value judgement of the writer, we cultivate a healthy distance between art object and artist. The goal is to free the artist to speak without fear of repercussion. To say, "That's offensive, not helpful, or irrelevant, and I want to move on," signals both authorial conviction and personal conviction. "You don't get free rein to speak to me that way" is a mantra worth inculcating in each and every one of our students.

I trust my workshop participants to honor the Lerman methodology, and in turn they hold themselves accountable and follow through. To gift them with this agency from the get-go incentivizes proving that they can be responsible and respectful workshop members. Of course, to set students up for success, we prepare ahead of time.

When a writer is up for workshop, we conference one-on-one in my office both before and after workshop. See chapter 7 for a step-by-step run down of these pre- and post-workshop conferences, but the gist is that the student sets an agenda and leads the meeting according to their most pressing concerns. Pre-workshop conferences might focus on last-minute edits to the workshop draft (that first, experimental attempt), airing out anxieties about sharing sensitive material, or tailoring the workshop methodology to best serve their individual needs (for example, brainstorming accommodations for students with slow processing speed or lack of reading fluency). Often, students will use their pre-workshop conference to discuss the artist statement assignment.

As a writer, I've always been fascinated by artist statements as means of relaying concept, inspiration, and process. I'm that person at the museum, reading the text on the wall before admiring the artwork. Why don't writers get an opportunity to share our approach alongside our art? To relay our vision is somehow taboo, for according to tradition, a writer's work must stand alone. "It's not like you'll be there when someone picks up your book," my peers used to admonish. Never mind that performance artists, visual and multimedia artists, directors, playwrights, and musicians all engage in some form of statement, from line notes to theatrical programs. What makes us so different?

And so, I adapted the Critical Response Process to include an artist statement. This is a typed, single-spaced, one-page letter from the writer to their fellow workshop participants. The letter includes a greeting, message, complimentary close, and signature. I love how the format familiarizes students with what one participant called "an ancient art form," while simultaneously deepening the reflection: Here is a writer's interpretation of the artist statement, intimate rather than formal, grounded in the personal and shared among community members. The letters are lovely works in and of themselves, honest and vulnerable and appreciative of their peers' time and energy. Note that the artist statement reverses the traditional power dynamic, in which writers receive letters from workshop participants. In the anti-racist model, it is the writer who initiates the dialogue.

After a student completes their workshop draft, I assign a long, lazy walk, a cup of tea, or a solid night's rest before writing the artist statement. The greater the distance, the better the result. My goal is to impede students from obsessive editing, inviting them to let go of the workshop draft, accept good enough, and shift their focus to reflection. The artist statement serves as the first page of their draft and includes responses to the following:

» Summarize your project in one to two sentences.

» What surprised you while you were crafting the project?

» What aspect(s) of the project posed the greatest challenge for you?

» What successes resulted from the project?

» What is your vision for future drafts?

» Enumerate three craft-based questions about your project to guide workshop discussion. What do you need help sorting out?

These reflection prompts draw on University of Iowa Professor Bonnie Sunstein's extensive writing about portfolios as personal literacy histories. Seeing as students rarely feel confident about their workshop draft, the artist statement allows space and time for the writer to gain perspective on their work, assessing the draft as a work in progress and registering aspects that went well. Beyond a portfolio of process, the statement serves to distance the writer emotionally from the draft before workshop so that they do not carry such heightened anxiety into the classroom (or if they do, at least we're all aware of and sympathetic to it).

Perhaps most importantly, the artist statement prepares students for step two of the Critical Response Process, Artist as Questioner. While the Lerman method offers opportunity for unlimited Q&A, I find that three solid questions are enough for the purposes of a workshop draft. Any more, and students have difficulty focusing on their revision goals. In our pre-workshop conference, students might choose to run drafts of their questions by me in order to ensure that they're clearly worded, craft-based, and neither too broad nor too narrow. Such careful preparation means that come workshop day, writers get the feedback they want and need to further their projects.

Empowering writers to listen to themselves by reflecting on their draft, facilitating their workshop, and moderating their peers' critique, is anti-racist work in action, a re-envisioning of the traditional model that best serves all students, but especially students of color.

Putting It All Together: Workshop

Colleagues are often surprised that I only offer one workshop per semester. It all depends on how you define "workshop." For example,
I dedicate the first month or two of class to low-stakes, daily opportunities to freewrite and read work aloud in order to bolster writers'
confidence and nurture communal trust. That's workshop, right?

Then, I transition into craft-based writing exercises (with a focus
on voice, imagery, characterization, and arrangement (aka "flow").
Students read these exercises aloud in small groups in an effort to
expose themselves to a variety of approaches and encourage future
experimentation. That's workshop, too.

In the weeks leading up to formal workshop, students bring
in drafts of their works in progress in order to dispel the myth of
perfection and ensure periodic advancement. They may share their
opening lines during check-in, step outside the classroom to record
themselves reading the draft aloud, or pair off and listen to their
words in someone else's mouth for perspective on what needs re-
finement. They may mark on their drafts during guided, large-group
editing sessions in pursuit of their writerly habits (paragraph and
sentence length, verb choice, "favorite" words, etc.). Other times we
might throw on some music and write en masse, warding off isolation and its pals, self-doubt, anxiety, despair, and procrastination.
That's workshop for sure.

By midpoint in the semester, students know one another's
names. They've championed one another's strengths and coached
each other's insecurities. Likely they've cried. Certainly, they've
laughed. Above all, they've witnessed each other grow in confidence and ability. When formal workshop rolls around, they're not
caught up in the social anxiety of whether or not the group will
judge them as "good" or "bad." It's just another opportunity to talk
about their work with mindfulness and compassion, curiosity and
camaraderie.

I allocate multiple weeks to formal workshop. Two to four
writers workshop per class period, depending on class length. Each

writer gets exactly thirty minutes to read their work aloud and then moderate their discussion. In the interest of time, writers distribute copies of their artist statement and draft before class begins, collated according to workshop order and placed on participants' seats. As a self-imposed reminder to rein in my impulse to control the conversation, I opt to sit in the back of the classroom, outside of the discussion circle.

We begin workshop by appealing to the senses: I spray lavender aromatherapy room mist to fight the funk and calm nerves. I play music as students enter the classroom. We share snack. On the board, I outline our adaptation of the Critical Response Process in case writers need help remembering the steps. Finally, I project our collective workshop vocabulary onto the wall as a prompt to keep our conversation craft-based.

Once everyone is seated, we silently read the writer's artist statement. Maybe the writer confides how fresh the material is or how sensitive the topic, and that they need encouragement to pursue later drafts with courage. Maybe the writer expresses that they have reached a dead end and feel like they're torturing the topic, and therefore need leads on what pops. Maybe the writer reveals certain cultural codes embedded in the text so as to inform the reader's experience, or else omits them altogether, designating an intended readership that "gets it." Whatever the writer chooses to communicate, the artist statement is an opportunity to engage in dialogue about the work before we experience the draft. It's guidance in how to most effectively approach the writing, and the writer. We conclude by studying the writer's three enumerated questions, our focal point for workshop feedback.

The writer starts a timing device (usually on their phone), greets everyone, and then proceeds to read their work aloud as participants follow on the page. Yes, the writer reads aloud, on the spot, in real time. No one takes the draft home the night before, scribbles all over it, and then crafts their critique into letter format. Rather than rehearsed analysis, participants' response is from the gut, in the moment. What moves you? Draw a check mark in the margins.

(As opposed to Lerman's specific, craft-based statements of meaning, check marks offer participants free rein to praise writers profusely.) What confuses you? Draw a question mark in the margins. I argue that this two-pronged, simplified feedback is enough to evolve an experimental workshop draft into a more fully realized first draft. It also restrains participants from succumbing to ego, writing their prescriptive opinions on or over the artist's words, going so far as to cross out sentences or slash whole paragraphs. "The workshop draft is but an attempt," I remind participants. "Copyediting comes later."

Oh, how my students balk at this move. Despite all of the unconventional exercises I've coaxed them into trying over the course of the class, reading their work aloud in formal workshop evokes the most protest. "How can we possibly read and critique in only 30 minutes?" they ask. I smile. "If you're worried about time constraints, you better practice efficiency." Too often students pound out pages to constitute a "draft," when really what they're doing is finding their way into (or out of) an essay, story, or play. We address the issue of length beforehand, in class discussion, peer-editing circles, and one-on-one conferences, so that students are better able to focus their draft into a manageable ten-to-twenty-minute excerpt.

You better believe that they time themselves reading the night before workshop to gauge the pace at which they'll need to moderate discussion. On rare occasions, a student will share their draft aloud for the full thirty minutes and that's an accomplishment in and of itself; workshop complete. More often, a student shares their draft and then negotiates the Critical Response Process with care, abridging or skipping steps to maximize their individual workshop experience.

In all of my years of teaching, students consistently marvel at how much they accomplish in the thirty-minute allotment. I credit this to Lerman's artist-centered methodology. When the writer is in control of the discussion, we no longer waste time on tangents, repetition, overly general praise, nitpicky details, or debate between respondents. I've had hour-and-a-half-long workshops and left with nothing substantial except the impulse to quit writing altogether.

I should note that the Critical Response Process looks different for every class. The week before formal workshops commence, students review Step One through Step Four and collectively decide which they'd like to keep as is and which they'd like to amend. Initially, students are game to attempt the methodology in full, after which we amend as we go. Sometimes workshop consists of Statements of Meaning and Artist Questions only. Sometimes we start with Neutral Questions, then lead into Artist Questions, then Statements of Meaning. When it comes to Permissioned Opinions, however, I don't budge. It's awkward to ask permission to express yourself, true, but it's downright agonizing to receive opinions without warning. A little heads-up helps.

The writer concludes workshop by thanking participants and then identifying one or more task points for revision. We call this *Step Five: Moving Forward.* It's satisfying as a responder to hear that your investment of time and energy has contributed to a writer's next move. Participants record their names on the writer's draft (allowing for follow-up questions), and then pass them forward for collection. Here I like to build in a short break before the next session begins so that we have time for a bathroom run, snack, or group stretch to sustain our endurance.

As I am physically removed from the discussion circle, I surrender the impulse to be the smartest person in the room, schooling students in how to write like me. Instead, I coach participants in the art of critique, observing their body language, engagement level, and word choice. I thank students for their generosity and sincerity and correct others who slipped into biased opinion. Of course, I congratulate the writer, as well. We schedule a one-on-one conference to evaluate their workshop experience, follow up on their peers' critique, and address any remaining questions about their draft.

Independent Workshopping

A staggered formal workshop schedule in which students share their drafts aloud in class means that there's no nightly homework, for students aren't reading and responding to one another's drafts in preparation for discussion. What are they doing, then?

Some of them write, while others revise. I call this independent workshopping.

I ask students early on in the semester to survey their individual writing habits. I preface by saying that every student enters workshop with a writing legacy, be it scribbled lyrics or love letters or thesis-driven essays. They don't need to identify as creative writers in order to analyze how they approach the page. Instead, the survey is an invitation to talk about process. Too often students assume that there's only one way to write, simply because they've always done it that way. The goal is to create awareness around how they currently use their time, compared to how they might want to use their time.

The survey includes questions like:

» What aspects of the writing process do you find most satisfying? Most challenging?

» What time of day do you write, and why?

» Where do you write, and why?

A common talking point is how to prevent distractions from sabotaging their writing sessions, transitioning students from a position of victimhood (This essay is ruining my life!) to a position of ownership (I've got a handle on my project). A realistic, nonjudgmental assessment of what drives them as writers helps students capitalize on their strengths and plan for their weaknesses.

Often, we as workshop leaders overlook revision as a writing habit, taking for granted that if we assign a post-workshop draft, students will contort themselves to meet that deadline on cue. How do we help students achieve agency between the workshop draft and the revised draft? In other words, how do we best position them to engage in independent workshopping?

The key is to meet them where they're at, creating a sense of ease and eliminating anxiety by allowing for individual choice. In the initial survey, I ask:

When you write, do you:

___ Revise immediately, sentence by sentence

___ Seek out a trusted reader to comment on installments of your draft

___ Wait to revise until you've finished the entire draft

___ Proofread before printing

___ Hold off on revisions entirely until you receive workshop feedback

What types of revisions do you do?

Small-scale revisions:

___ Eliminate typos

___ Modify grammar and/or punctuation

___ Enhance word choice

___ Correct inconsistencies

___ Smooth transitions for overall polish

Large-scale revisions:

___ Strengthen the overall cohesion

___ Rework organization

___ Develop existing ideas

___ Deepen purpose or "stakes"

___ Tackle structural changes

___ Experiment with stylistic changes

___ Write new content

Are you happy with your revision process? Do you find it effective?

If you could change some aspect of it, what would you change?

Obviously, this is an excellent opportunity to talk about revision. What do the above terms even mean, and how do students go about executing these moves on the page? Beyond exposure to different revision techniques, an honest assessment of their revision habits allows for opportunity to map out a workshop schedule that best serves their process—or better yet, envision a healthier approach, implementing steps toward personal change.

When students sign up for a workshop slot, we return to these early surveys. Do they write messy, experimental drafts, and need time to slowly work through their ideas in the revision stage? These students claim the early workshop dates. Do they enjoy a slow writing process, and feed off of the pressure to revise quickly? If so, then they claim a later workshop date. In this way, I aim to tailor the revision assignment to best suit their individual needs, as opposed to imposing my own expectations of what they should achieve, and by when.

Risking a Better Way

It's not easy to adapt our creative and cultural heritage. It will likely feel uncomfortable at first, for both you and your students. Maybe no one else in your program wants change. Maybe it's you who is hesitant to let go. Maybe your students inadvertently misstep the course of action and want to revert to the traditional model.

Stick with it.

Don't give in.

To give in is to devolve.

Let's risk a better way, one that heeds the humanity of writers of color. Eboo Patel teaches, "To see the other side, to defend another people, not despite your tradition but because of it, is the heart of pluralism."[9]

It is up to you to release control. Control and dominance are trademarks of the traditional writing workshop and, by extension, white supremacy. Surrender to an alternative model that might feel less safe to you and safer to every single workshop participant of color under your mentorship for the remainder of your teaching career. This is not to say that your concerns don't have value, they're just outranked in the anti-racist configuration.

Dr. Beverly Daniel Tatum has this great metaphor for racism as an airport's moving walkway in her book *"Why Are All the Black Kids Sitting Together in the Cafeteria?" And Other Conversations about Race*:

Active racist behavior is equivalent to walking fast on the conveyor belt. The person engaged in active racist behavior has identified with the ideology of white supremacy and is moving with it. Passive racist behavior is equivalent to standing still on the walkway. No overt effort is being made, but the conveyor belt moves the bystanders along to the same destination as those who are actively walking. Some of the bystanders may . . . choose to turn around, unwilling to go to the same destination as the white supremacists. But unless they are walking actively in the opposite direction at a speed faster than the conveyor belt—unless they are actively antiracist—they will find themselves carried along with the others.[10]

To do nothing is to stand still and submit to white supremacy. Take action.

CHAPTER SEVEN

Conferencing as Critique

Culturally Relevant Teaching

I held down my first classroom at nineteen years old. I was an AmeriCorps volunteer who led writing workshops at Roberto Clemente High School in Chicago's Humboldt Park. AmeriCorps has since done away with the high school program in favor of a middle school focus, likely because we volunteers were only a year or two older than our students and therefore prone to wildly inappropriate interactions. It wasn't rare to lose a colleague overnight. "Where's Jeremy?" I'd ask, only to get that knowing look that meant that Jeremy had sold weed to a student or got high with a student or had sex with a student. Our bright red coats and Timberland khakis may have sped us through the school's metal detector line with faculty favoritism, but the uniform wasn't enough to change who we were on the inside: kids.

The Clemente students tolerated us, thank god. They'd gather in our fishbowl office in between classes or after school, uniformed themselves in white t-shirts and jeans. Where else was there to go, really? Outside, a police car parked diagonally across the sidewalk, a fixture at the front doors; inside, makeshift classrooms made it hard to move, stacked chairs and duct-taped textbooks crowding the hallways. The students sought us out and we talked and talked about b-boys and eyebrow threading and the cousin who was shot last night by a rival gang in front of their house.

They deserved better than our patchwork team of five, drifters from across the country who chose a year of full-time volunteerism to escape or absolve or enhance ourselves. They deserved better than me, private school kid whose poker face held firm despite the shock I felt at the disparity of their educational access. How easy it must be for teachers to marginalize these students, I thought, to pity and patronize them as Other, deserving of a lesser standard because they wouldn't, or couldn't, try harder. But the students did try. They showed up, and they spoke up, opened up. What mattered was that we empathized enough to listen, to understand that talking is the foundation of writing. The page came second as a source of relief; we got to that later.

These on-the-fly conversations served me well after Ameri-Corps as I transitioned back into college, supporting myself with work as a private tutor. Wealthy white parents posted ads on DePaul University's education bulletin board, aiming for an accomplished graduate student to supervise their child's nightly homework. It was me who answered their call, undergraduate English major who hustled hard. I'd arrive early on their manicured thresholds, smiling as they escorted the previous interviewee out the door (white women much taller than me, with grown-up purses and kitten-heeled shoes). Make no mistake, the market was competitive, but it came down to this: "Maddie just insisted we hire you," the mother would tell me later, over the phone. "She took to you immediately." I'd get the job, not because I was especially qualified (I wasn't), but because I knew how to talk to their children.

These mothers were quick to inventory their child's learning challenges, for they were trying as hard as they could, they just needed extra support. Support in the form of sun-soaked private school classrooms, specialized assignments sensitive to their individual advancement, an organizational coach to balance the demands of a middle school curriculum, and me, an in-home private tutor.

Shocking, the disparity of their educational access, but my expression never betrayed me. I'd sit atop overstuffed couches sipping San Pellegrino, devising how best to champion the child's success.

One-on-one with the kids was a different story. "This is stupid. I need to go to the bathroom. I need a snack. Show me, please, just this once? Do it for me. Then I'll know how." The trick was in the talking. They thought it got them out of doing homework, and so they'd tell me about their interests and hobbies. With time, I was able to merge the two, pivoting between nightly learning standards and their particular learning styles. We'd sketch an essay as a comic, make math rules into rhymes, or turn a reading response into a ball game, with laundry baskets serving as multiple choice options. With enough talking, we'd get to the heart of it: "This is stupid" became "I'm stupid," a belief they clung to despite their mothers' inexhaustible reassurances to the contrary. It was from here, a place of openness, that we could truly progress (see chapter 2).

Eventually I'd burn out, resentful of the family's assumption of my constant availability. I was yet another of their things: cashmere scarf strewn on the staircase and bootstamped wet, steak dinner abandoned on the granite countertop. I remember coveting one family's hand soap so severely that I pocketed it upon quitting as though it were due to me, taxes for having to remind them, again, that they forgot to pay me. I'd lay low in my studio apartment for a week or two, savoring my autonomy, and then it was on to the next hustle.

It was the nonprofit arts organization Young Chicago Authors (YCA) that taught me that what I was doing—dialogue as educational practice—wasn't a hustle at all, but an art form called culturally relevant teaching. When you let students lead, when you invite them to talk and you explicitly listen to them, you nurture their critical consciousness. As opposed to the traditional practice of inserting culture into education, culturally relevant teaching inserts education into the culture, thus humanizing learning.[1] Beyond a foundation in reading and writing, what you're really cultivating is voice, the skillset necessary to speak "in"—articulating ideas, hopes, and fears—and then to speak "out"—renouncing inequitable systems at play in students' own lives and the lives of others. Inherent to this anti-racist art form is the belief that young people are experts of their own experiences.

Back then, YCA was a glorified treehouse perched high on Division Avenue, a quick couple of blocks from Clemente High School: a second-floor apartment with a ramshackle kitchen and mismatched couches. I knew the nonprofit organization well from my year with AmeriCorps, having attended their spoken word poetry open mic series with my students. YCA was the opposite of school, a refuge for teenagers who loved to write and the talented teaching artists who were down to mentor them.

Come my senior year of college, I had no doubt in my mind that I would work at YCA. As it turns out, they hired me, largely because I kept showing up. "Nah, we're good on volunteers," a staff member told me over the phone, but I volunteered anyway, stuffing envelopes alongside board members, scrubbing toilets after hours, substitute teaching at a moment's notice. To every request I answered, "Yes, absolutely, of course," even if most of the time I had no idea what I was doing. Eventually, I evolved into a teaching artist, then an office manager, and finally a program manager.

I credit the organization as my foundation in a democratic education, a model of teaching that didn't necessitate police presence or private tutoring, but a human-to-human connection: students and mentors in dynamic dialogue. Guidance, motivation, and emotional support proved to be the end game, so different from the pressure to try your hardest. Try your hardest according to whom? To achieve what? We weren't out to get writing "right." We wanted to make writing relevant to the writer.

Workshop leaders, what might you learn if you invert hierarchy and listen instead of lecture? More to the point, what might your listening teach your workshop participants about their own inherent value as scholars, artists, and citizens? This chapter advises you to put down the red pen—or, better yet, to put it in the hand of the writer. Instead of scribbling on participants' work, prescribing alternate grammar, phrasing, or narrative strategies that align with your personal aesthetic preferences, consider guided pre- and post-work-shop conferences. Through open dialogue, you center participants in their learning experience.

Ditching the Hatchet

Student conferences are an alternate form of critique that is entirely verbal, a means of editing participants' work that is both student-centered and student-administered. Each conference occurs at a strategic juncture in the creative process—just before and just after formal workshop—when you as workshop leader tend to have the most influence. The point is to relinquish control of the conversation.

To be clear, I didn't always work this way. Just ask my friend Ben, who in high school sought me out as a peer editor because he felt safe with me, only to bark an astonished laugh when I returned his personal essay, the type illegible under my scrawl. "Did you like any of it?" he asked, his mouth smiling but his eyes dull. I'd go on to earn the nickname "The Hatchet" among my writer friends, as so little of their text survived my read.

I wanted, in effect, to write their work for them.

I could exert such control in these informal exchanges, but once I started teaching university classes, it became more and more time consuming for me to rewrite my students' work via "grading." All that effort to inspire an egalitarian classroom community, undone by my axe work on the page! I couldn't see it then, how I was undermining my own anti-racist practice; I thought my meticulous edits made me a model teacher. "I'm taking my students seriously," I said to myself, even though it was me dominating the exchange.

I remember sitting at my green Formica table surrounded by stacks of essays, watching the sun dash the sky through the kitchen window, each passing hour provoking a suffocating dread. I tried arranging students' papers into a hierarchy of "worst" to "best" so that I tackled the most complex edits first (an admission that shames me now). I tried timing myself: a strict one hour per essay (and even then I was racing to beat the clock). I tried relocating to a cafe (the logic being that my longing for pajamas and a pint of ice cream would undermine my impulse to "improve" students' work).

I began to hate grading, or at least my treatment of student work. My motivation for change was selfish: How can I make this more pleasurable?

I started by asking students to indicate on their drafts what sort of feedback they'd prefer, a request that required them to reflect on their individual writing process. Were they toying with new ideas or techniques and wanted encouragement? Were they expelling a messy draft in hopes of discovering what pops? Were they finalizing a draft for publication and wanted line edits? Just because all of my students completed an identical assignment didn't mean that their relationship to the work was identical. Why was I treating their drafts as such? Looking back, I see that this attempt to bring the writer into the work was an early iteration of the artist statement. With a human connection and an identifiable purpose for me to fulfill, my engagement with their writing stopped eliciting such dread.

Still, it was hard to squash my compulsion to control the text. Was it the physical stance of holding pen to paper, I wondered, that triggered my ego?

What if I put the pen down?

Soon I was recording audio files of myself talking about each student's work on my cell phone. I devised parameters: I could inventory unlimited successes, but only suggest three major points of consideration for revision. This meant no nitpicky asides, as I was accustomed to giving on the page. And because I needed shareable file sizes suitable to e-mail, I had to cut myself short while recording, thwarting any perfectionistic impulses to word my feedback just so. "Keep it casual," I told myself, "like you're having a conversation."

Audio critique cut my grading time in half, but more so, it preserved the integrity of workshop participants' texts. Their words remained intact on the page, with only my voice to guide them, should they seek me out.

One day, a student complained that she never received my audio file. I'd sent it, I was sure of it, but after searching her inbox and spam folder, we confirmed that it was indeed missing. I panicked. I'd taken to deleting the files after e-mailing them to prevent overwhelming my cell phone memory. It was gone. What would I do?

"Couldn't we just, you know, talk?" the student asked.

It was in that moment that I realized my audio files were nothing more than a one-sided conversation, yet another means of exerting control. Why not ditch the hatchet and invite workshop participants into a dialogue about their work?

"Oh, right," I said. "Of course. Let's talk."

Conference as Collaboration

When I quiz students, "What are three things you would request of your workshop leader to enable you to produce your best work?," they tend to go mute. They weren't aware that they were allowed to ask anything of me, beyond a critical read. To that end, I advocate that my students be the ones to conduct the pre- and post-workshop conferences. For me, this was the final step in relinquishing control: allowing the writer to lead the conversation.

Such leadership requires preparation. The week before their workshop date, students sign up for a twenty-minute, one-on-one conference. ("Twenty minutes!" they balk, but that's before I educate them in effective use of time management.) To ensure a productive meeting, workshop participants prepare the following in advance of their conference, usually as an in-class freewriting exercise:

» What does your draft need right now? Be specific. Craft an agenda of your three most pressing writing needs in order of urgency to help guide the conversation.

» How might your workshop leader contribute to your writing needs? Identify a short list of explicit actions, making it easy for your workshop leader to contribute.

» What do you need right now, on an emotional level? How can you untangle your writing needs from your emotional needs before your conference so that you're fully present and open to receiving feedback?

This reflective exercise encourages students to actively assess their mindset in advance of their pre-workshop conference, giving voice to the technical, creative, and emotional needs surrounding their work. Too often, students passively receive their workshop leader's feedback, only to suffer an emotional backlash of responses they wish they would have said, questions they wish they would have asked, or feelings they don't know how to process outside of labeling themselves as "good" or "bad" at writing. By taking an active role in conferencing, workshop participants are better able to channel their emotions into points of action.

Once they've surveyed their mindset, students' next task is to create parameters for their pre-workshop conference so that they get the most out of the twenty-minute meeting. To that end, participants prepare agendas:

» List three specific, guiding questions to generate dialogue about your work. Your questions can range from last-minute edits to your workshop draft, anxieties about sharing sensitive work, talking through the workshop methodology one more time to ensure understanding, or rehearsing your artist statement questions. Maybe you have your eye on a particular publishing venue. Maybe you want to troubleshoot ethical considerations. The point is that you are in charge of your time. You can use it as you see fit.

» Arrange the questions so that you lead with your most pressing concern. That way, if time should run out, you're certain to have covered the main talking points.

» Type your agenda. Print two copies (one for you and one for your workshop leader) and bring them with you to the meeting.

» Come prepared with a timing device so that you may proceed through your agenda while regulating the time.

» Finally, take notes during the meeting. Remember, your workshop leader's feedback is entirely verbal. It is up to you to extract action points from the conversation.

Note that the students are active participants in their pre-workshop conferences, which serves to bolster their confidence, heighten the productivity of meetings, and allow for a healthy separation of work and well-being. The workshop leader provides feedback, but it's framed within the context of the student's guiding questions, condensing critique into focused, manageable doses. The critical choices, moving forward, belong to the writer alone.

When I've shared this approach in one-on-one and departmental training sessions, workshop leaders often ask, "But what if I want to say something in the pre-workshop conference that's not on my student's agenda? Something glaring. An easy fix." My advice is to say nothing. Sit on it until workshop. If the writer invites your permissioned opinion, then you may share your insights. To do otherwise is a self-serving violation of the conference ethos.

Remember, you're discouraging the routine practice of pounding out pages to please the workshop leader. Together you reframe conferences as a collaboration, prompting the student to acknowledge their own accountability. The pre-workshop conference is a reversal of power: Students claim ownership of not only their writing, but their working relationship with the workshop leader.

Post-workshop conferences serve to fulfill a different purpose. These meetings occur directly after students' formal workshop, or else the following day. Capped at twenty minutes, students make use of the post-workshop conference in myriad of ways:

» How would you evaluate the quality of your workshop experience?

» What aspects of your peers' critique would you like clarity on?

» How might you deepen your understanding of a particular craft element in relation to your draft?

» What remaining questions do you have about your work?

» What is your plan of action, moving forward?

The spirit of these sessions is celebratory and impromptu—there's no set agenda, just the student taking time to reflect on a milestone in the creative process. Reading one's work aloud is a big deal, after all. Sometimes we use the full twenty minutes just to revel in the success of the workshop or the draft. My hope is that no one exits my office burdened by ambiguity or insult as a result of their writing workshop.

If, during the post-workshop conference, a student wants my opinion on an aspect of their draft, I ensure that I, too, adhere to the Lerman methodology. This means that during workshop, I read the draft in real time, noting check marks and question marks. I might vocalize statements of meaning that the group leaves unsaid, or else jot them down in my notebook to share later in conference. I record my own responses to the writer's three craft questions in my notebook (especially responses that deviate from the group consensus) and then note any questions that I have about the draft. That way, I am prepared should the student seek out my advice. If I feel compelled to introduce a personal opinion, I make sure to request the student's permission during conference (though admittedly, they rarely decline).

Pausing to reflect on the writing workshop experience benefits the student by allowing them to process their experience aloud, thus validating their internal conversation. It benefits the class as a whole by commemorating what aspects of the workshop went well and targeting opportunities for improvement, thus developing their higher-level thinking and problem solving. And it benefits the workshop leader by allowing for deep listening, fostering a sense of connection to and deeper awareness of each and every student.

Exercising voice isn't just a matter for the page. It's also an essential skill in connecting with others to build just, healthy, and more sustainable communities. I advocate that you empower your workshop participants to take charge of their projects by teaching them the managerial skills that best serve long-term, collaborative projects. While these skills might diverge from academia's traditional, product-based methodology of research, writing, and revision, they do serve to support a holistic, process-based methodology in which workshop participants aim to please themselves, taking pride in the leadership their writing entailed.

Cost-Benefit Analysis

When I preach the advantages of pre- and post-workshop conferences to writing teacher colleagues, the vibe in the room is a tangible "Oh hell no!" I know what they're thinking. Meet with every student one-on-one, twice? Who has time for all that?

I don't back down so easily.

True, the twenty-minute conferences add up, especially when you're teaching multiple sections simultaneously. But have you ever assessed how you currently use your time? Calculate the following:

» The amount of time you spend e-mailing back and forth with students who have "a quick question about my draft" before workshop

» The amount of time you spend reading student work outside of the classroom

» The amount of time you spend crafting responses to student work outside of the classroom

» The amount of time you spend e-mailing back and forth with students who have "a quick question about my draft" after workshop

» The amount of time you spend following up with students via office hour consultations clarifying your responses to their work

Calculate and compare: forty minutes total per student for pre- and post-workshop conferences that consist entirely of verbal critique. This means that you never take student work home. Conferences engender a healthier you, literally (as in, you don't constantly catch colds from germ-ridden pages), and figuratively, in that you cultivate respectful, supportive relationships with your students.

"But how does it work, exactly?" colleagues want to know.

Depending on your academic calendar, formal workshop can span between one week to a month or more. Each class session features between two and four writers, on average. Say, for example, that you workshop two students per class twice a week on Tuesdays and Thursdays. This translates into eight one-on-one meetings: four pre-workshop conferences and four post-workshop conferences. Your schedule would look like this:

> **MONDAY:** Two pre-workshop conferences with students A and B for a total of forty minutes.
>
> **TUESDAY:** Formal in-class workshop of students A and B, followed by two post-workshop conferences, for a total of forty minutes.
>
> **WEDNESDAY:** Two pre-workshop conferences with students C and D for a total of forty minutes.
>
> **THURSDAY:** Formal in-class workshop of students C and D, followed by two post-workshop conferences, for a total of forty minutes.
>
> **FRIDAY:** Open for contingencies.

Broken down as such, that's one extra hour per day, per class, each week during formal workshop.

If conferences still sound like too much of a time sap, you might consider blocking out the week before formal workshop as "Independent Writing," substituting classes for one-on-one meetings. This works best for truncated academic schedules or if you're teaching multiple sections simultaneously. Personally, I find these marathon conferencing sessions exhausting, but they certainly free up time when there's none to spare. Just remember to schedule in bathroom breaks! In a pinch, I've pulled students out of class one by one to conference while others engage in an editing exercise, or else conducted conferences over the phone from home (which is surprisingly enjoyable, plus I get to wear slippers).

Key to the success of these conferences is safeguarding your time so that you are truly available and present for your writers. I let my class know in advance that come formal workshop, my e-mail accessibility and office hours are reserved for that week's writers only. If others have a question about their drafts, they either note it on their pre-conference agenda, or rely on one another for support (I promote out-of-class, small group troubleshooting sessions, what students and I informally call "shitty first draft groups" after Anne Lamott's *Bird by Bird*).

While it might sound like a gargantuan task to meet with every writer before and after workshop, in reality, you're gifting yourself time consolidation. There are firm boundaries to your accessibility, so your workshop participants must plan ahead to make the most out of each exchange. They have to take initiative in their own education.

It is the student who administers the pre-workshop conference, so there's no need for you to prepare talking points in advance.

It is the student who reads their writing aloud during workshop, so there's no need for you to pore over the draft at home.

It is the student who articulates guiding questions about their writing, so there's no need for you to dominate class discussion.

It is the student who elicits specific, craft-based feedback on their draft, so there's no need for you to impulsively edit according to your personal aesthetic preferences.

It is the student who reflects on the quality of that feedback, posing follow-up questions in the post-workshop conference, so there's no need for you to field long-winded e-mails deciphering their peers' critique.

Finally, it is the student who chooses which edits they will pursue in a revised draft, so there's no need for you to articulate their writing goals for them.

What do you do?

You try as hard as you can to listen.

You try as hard as you can to receive.

You try as hard as you can to empower.

CHAPTER EIGHT

Promoting Camaraderie and Collective Power

Academic Freedom

When I first started teaching at Colorado College, I was thrilled at the prospect of my own office. Two years as a full-time caregiver to my son taught me that a room with a door that locked was a crucial coping strategy—better than, say, crying into my ham sandwich at the park. That's why I didn't flinch when my supervisor led me up one flight of stairs, away from my new colleagues, toward a small, hot, windowless room. "There was really nothing else," she apologized. "Tech will be by soon to set up your computer."

I smiled in the ensuing silence. My office!

Three taps on the door signaled Tech, a bald white guy with pierced ears and my desktop computer. "They stuck in you here?" he asked, frowning. "This is an old storage closet." And then, after a pause, "You really don't rate, do you?"

What could I say? He was kind of killing my high.

"You know who they put in places like these? People the college wants to forget about."

At that, he left.

I felt suddenly flushed, the silence crushing. Little did I know, the quiet wouldn't last.

The office next to mine belonged to an ombudsman, a white, male conflict resolution practitioner with whom faculty and staff sorted out their workplace disputes. I know this because the connecting wall between our offices was so thin that I could hear every word of their exchanges. At first, the writer in me perked at such private conversations: white men and women affronted by accusations of racist or sexist behavior. I kept a running Word doc of phrases that materialized in the muggy air around me: My alleged insensitivity. These zealous activists. Bunch of student snowflakes. Whatever happened to academic freedom?

Was this what it was like to pass, I wondered, that cloak of invisibility, white folks unguarded among themselves? I was one wall removed from the racist campus culture I knew existed and yet I couldn't call it out. Neither could I tune it out.

Good God, the irony. At the time I was mentoring a student who planned to petition the college for greater diversity in curricular content and pedagogical strategies. When she and other students of color sought me out to discuss classroom experiences of racist and sexist bigotry, I found myself talking a little louder than necessary. Maybe our message would carry over the wall?

Eventually I went to my supervisor and complained. The whole ombuds business was stressing me out. It wasn't my job to hear out their nonsense. Which made me wonder, why could I hear it at all? Weren't these conversations meant to be confidential? Why stick the ombuds rep in a closet?

That is, after all, where the college puts people they want to forget about.

"We, the students of Colorado College, believe that every student who graduates from CC should have a basic grasp of issues concerning responsible citizenship in a globalized world," began students' open letter to the school administration. "This petition is a formal statement of our dedication to engaging with subjects of (but not limited to) class, race, gender, and sexuality everyday—

subjects we want to see reflected in our classrooms and in syllabi across campus."[1]

More and more, students nationwide are harnessing their collective power to expose closeted issues of racial animus. They write letters. Long, eloquent, researched letters claiming their citizenship and demanding plurality. This is evidence of anti-racist writing at its finest: the skillset necessary to turn inward—divulging personal narratives of subjugation—and outward—channeling those narratives into change.

They're calling us out.

No longer can we actively deny institutional, structural, and individual racism in our colleges and universities. To do so is both academically irresponsible and morally abhorrent. Our students are calling us out because they know that without public pressure for comprehensive change, academia's legacy of systemic racism will persist.

"You cannot afford to ignore the problems festering in your department, in your classrooms, and in your colleagues' classrooms," writes a group of Williams College students in their open letter to the school administration. Their campaign, #BoycottEnglish, is clear: "We refuse to be forced out of our classrooms by misogyny and racism any longer."[2]

"We are dismayed by the many white supremacist, anti-Semitic, sexist, and anti-LGBTQ messages that have been posted, painted, carved, or otherwise displayed in dorms, classrooms, campus buildings, and online," writes University of Nevada, Reno students in their open letter to the school administration. "You leave marginalized students and their supporters to carry the burden for transforming the campus climate, while at the same time, restricting their ability to do so."[3]

"We call on current Yale leaders to move beyond the insufficient promises of neoliberal diversity and inclusion," writes Black graduate students and allies in their open letter to the school administration. "Fostering inclusivity for people of color is important, but demanding a protocol which ensures accountability for unnecessary and antagonistic actions taken against people of color is imperative for implementing true systemic change."[4]

"We are tired of doing the work to feel safe, because the school consistently fails to provide us safety," writes Franklin & Marshall students in their open letter to the school administration. "We and our allies have come together to demand that Franklin & Marshall's administration implement immediate and lasting changes to halt intolerable and continuous acts of racism that students of color endure at the College."[5]

And on and on.

It's time to come out of the closet, y'all. Education is no longer a matter of rote regurgitation: Here's what you told me to do and so I did it. Our students want to know why, and to what end. They want the tools necessary to stake a claim in more just, equitable, and inclusive learning communities. That's real academic freedom.

Our classrooms can nurture these citizens, if we so choose. We can teach them to act with moral courage and intellectual honesty by rejecting traditions of cultural assimilation and suppression. We can show them what it is to reclaim, revitalize, and reimagine what education looks like by modeling anti-racist workshops that value voice. To each and every student we can say, "You matter."

Colorado College is doing just that, spearheading an institutional initiative toward transformational change. The administration's sweeping nine-point strategy aims to position the college at the leading edge of racial justice in higher education. The first step? Acknowledging that racism exists, for it can't be addressed if it's not talked about. President Jill Tiefenthaler writes in her letter to the campus community, "Racism has existed at Colorado College since our founding, and it still exists today . . . we have to shift gears, taking up the work of antiracism, which means we actively oppose racism in all of its forms. I truly believe that this effort is crucial to changing higher education and the world for the better."[6] Key to the success of the initiative is accountability: Each and every member of the college must contribute toward change. From there, progress is collective, urgent, and active.

The end game is shifting. Today's young people demand an education that is as much about equity and power as it is about reading and writing. As such, we must reevaluate our own course assessment strategies. How do we define success? The tradition of ranking workshop participants based on implicit bias fails our students of color, effectively pushing them out of the classroom. Instead, workshop leaders should aim for the heart of discovery:

» Who were you when you began this journey?

» What did you set out to do, and why?

» Where are you currently in your learning?

» What's next?

This sort of discovery-based assessment is unique to each student, allowing for authentic engagement, understanding, and growth. It allows for hope on a lasting personal level, beyond the confines of the classroom. When participants believe that they have real voice, hope trumps any arbitrary letter grade. It is this hope that is essential to our change makers.

"When we begin to become tired and discouraged, when hopelessness seems just around the corner, and when we wonder what good our actions are doing, we need to remind ourselves of the strengths and assets we possess," writes Dr. Derald Wing Sue in his "Open Letter to Brothers and Sisters of Color." He goes on to illustrate what strength looks like in action:

> We have survived through our collective strength. We have survived through our heightened perceptual wisdom. We have survived through our ability to read the contextualized meanings of our oppressors. We have survived through our bicultural flexibility. We have survived through our families and communities. We have survived through our spirituality and our religion. We have survived through our racial/ethnic identity and pride. We have survived through our belief in the interconnectedness of the human condition.[7]

Such resiliency in the face of oppression may not register as success according to traditional, top-down models of assessment, just as our students' tireless petitions to dismantle white supremacy are not worthy of college credit. But if we shift our perception of what constitutes learning—if we change the means of assessment to a more human, discovery-based model—suddenly your students of color have opportunity to flourish.

This chapter encourages workshop participants to assess their creativity as a process of surrender, not control. Control is key to the traditional model: Bend your words to satisfy the workshop leader, to get a good grade, to earn an invitation to read aloud. Instead of outward, workshop participants go inward with perspective and intention to gauge their personal progress.

Assessment as Learning

A few years back, I had a student who sought me out during office hours. He placed his workshop draft and his revised draft side by side on my desk. "Here," he said, pointing to a scene on the fourth page. "Right here. You're really excited about it the first time around, and then confused by it in my revision."

I stared at the pages. He was absolutely right. I'd unintentionally switched my stance on the exact same material. In all my years of teaching, no one had ever presented me with evidence of my inconsistency, though I'm sure it's happened often enough.

"Huh," I said, because I had nothing else to offer. It's awful to admit, but every now and then I totally blank during conference. My brain just won't cooperate.

"Maybe it's the difference between hearing it aloud and then reading it on the page?" I offered, but he just stared at me. He knew he deserved better.

I sighed. "Well, what does it matter what I think anyway? I obviously can't be trusted."

He flinched.

"Okay, okay. Pretend you're the teacher. What would you say?"

"Um, I guess I would ask what I wanted from the scene? Like, what's its purpose? Does it move the essay forward?" He then went on to answer his questions, one by one, making a solid case for keeping the essay intact.

This is the difference between assessment of learning versus assessment as learning. Because if I'd gone ahead and graded his essay according to a traditional methodology (I didn't understand this scene, so change it), I would've missed out on an opportunity to experience his thinking, how this particular scene reflected an application of skills he'd set out to test in workshop. Our role reversal didn't fluster him in the least because by that point in the workshop, he was well accustomed to setting his own goals and monitoring his own progress.

We both knew I was far from infallible. Why put me in charge of judging his personal evolution as a writer?

Four years later, long after he'd graduated from the college, I received an e-mail from this student. "It was allowing myself to take some risks and leaps in your class that all of a sudden made things click," he wrote, reflecting on our workshop together. "While I am proud of what I achieved, I do feel that the culture of support and caring you created and the way you pushed us to focus on questions rather than answers allowed me to access a part of me that now feels fundamental."

This is what we're aiming for. Learning that lasts.

How do we get there?

We start by acknowledging that our workshop participants are experts in their own right. Early on in class, survey them as a means to better scaffold them later on:

» What is your name? *You have the right to claim space.*

» Where do you come from? *You are endowed with a storytelling legacy.*

» Who are your artistic mentors? *Your knowledge is legitimate.*

» What do you fear? *You are in a safe space.*

» What do you want? *You are free to risk failure.*

» Why are you good at writing? *You are, and have always been, a writer.*

I dole out these questions as a series of freewrites over the first week or two of class, requiring every student to stand and read their responses aloud. Beyond a means of introduction, this initial survey serves to differentiate participants' interests and learning preferences. Moving forward, they set their own learning goals to best serve their specific needs, and I tailor my teaching to best support them.

Considering that so much of writing is psychological, students' earliest self-assessments center on fear. My strategy is to debunk the myth of the muse at the get-go. The more we publicly articulate the hardships of writing, the more receptive students are to the discovery process, collectively brainstorming strategies for success (see chapter 2). The key is for students to realize that they aren't the only one who struggles, that fallacy we tend toward when isolated for too long.

Together we acknowledge that writing is an inherently imperfect, ongoing process fraught with insecurity. Afraid of sounding stupid? Write anyway. Afraid of sharing something private? Write anyway. Afraid of imperfection? Write anyway. With time and attention, students can work to individually and collectively conquer their fears. This means setting an intention as a group to grow. "We facilitated a beautiful sense of community," writes a former student, "built on mutual trust and respect, where we were able to share our work, get feedback from each other, bounce ideas around, talk ideas through that we couldn't fully form ourselves, and try things we wouldn't otherwise be brave enough to try. Becoming a stronger writer was a process of reciprocation. Once I held up my end of the deal by opening up and sharing more vulnerable excerpts of my writing, the class was able to give me real feedback and direction." Such vulnerability results in a close-knit community of trust.

"How do you arrive at something worth gathering about?" asks Priya Parker in *The Art of Gathering: How We Meet and Why It*

Matters. "What are the ingredients for a sharp, bold, meaningful gathering purpose?"[8] Too often the manner in which we convene doesn't connect with students on a personal level, and so they end up bored, stuck on autopilot. Too often the purpose of the course is to please the workshop leader in order to earn a good grade. When you set the stakes for something meaningful to occur, suddenly students are invested: This isn't about a grade, this is about transformation. Parker prompts us to move from the what (a creative nonfiction writing workshop) to the why (challenging your fear so that you may exercise voice and claim your citizenship). There's risk involved, and that risk is the first step in a discovery-based model of learning.

Our Own Best Assessors

Back when I was a grad student, a professor distributed a photocopied packet of everyone's writing—short, two-to-three-page essays that we'd written the week before. He asked us to silently read the essay of the person sitting next to us, then act as a "gatekeeper" for their work. Which essay was the best, he asked. Which was the worst? It was horrible to point a finger at someone else and say "bad." Many of us chose not to. I promised myself that when I taught, I would never do the same to my students.

Still, your workshop participants "know." They intuit who are the "best" and "worst" writers in the room according to the workshop leader's social cues. Praise that goes on a little too long, a little too often. A sigh of disinterest, a forced compliment. While a far cry from my grad school indictment, workshop leaders are in the habit of comparing students against one another and then ranking them. Students follow suit, contorting their writing to earn top tier.

Assuming you're favored, this traditional method of assessment reaps rewards. Public praise. A high grade. An invitation to read at the end-of-term celebration, an invitation to apply for the "advanced" course. Publication in the college literary journal. And the confidence to claim the identity of writer.

Must I say it, whose essay a white peer deemed the worst that day? A Black woman.

If you're not favored, there's resounding pressure from the workshop leader to stop writing, to silence yourself.

I will not be silenced.

I will not silence my students of color.

A discovery-based model of assessment reallocates power from the workshop leader to the workshop participant. They claim their inherent worth as a writer—that's just a given. No more pointing fingers, "good" or "bad." Instead, assessment is individualized and fluid, a critical awareness of one's ever-changing self over the course of the term.

To teach students how to be their own best assessors, you must provide frequent opportunities for practice. Rather than the traditional, top-down model in which workshop leaders assess participants en masse at the end of class, a discovery-based model incorporates periodic, multi-tier opportunities for self-assessment throughout the term:

Inward Reflection: Low-stakes freewriting exercises ask participants to reflect on what they are risking by exercising voice. What do they want from their writing? What do they want from reading their work aloud? The resulting narratives provide a starting point from which workshop participants can gauge their growth. Such freewriting heightens engagement, safety, and trust within the collective.

Connecting with the Body: The daily ritual of check-in, coupled with sequenced mindfulness exercises, reminds workshop participants to fully inhabit their bodies. How can they align who they are, and how they feel, with the day's anti-racist workshop agenda? Connecting with oneself emboldens workshop participants to value their voice. Eventually this practice transcends outward to valuing one another in creative community, fostering a culture of dignity and respect.

Monitoring Their Own Progress: Individualized writing prompts and self-selected reading assignments mean that workshop participants have voice in their own learning, empowering individual identity exploration. Students choose to adhere to a firm attendance policy, manage ongoing Task Lists to ensure progress on their projects, and share their raw work aloud in an effort to remain accountable to their creative purpose.

Setting Individual Goals: Moderating their own feedback sessions and one-on-one conferences teaches participants how to think, rather than simply what to think. They analyze their creative output and craft agendas about their own work—independent of the workshop leader's influence—using a vocabulary of craft concepts that they themselves defined. Setting their own goals increases students' critical thinking skills and enhances their self-confidence.

Providing Feedback to One Another: In-class opportunities to listen to, read, and/or respond to one another's work in partner, small group, and large group workshops nurtures empathy and increases cultural competence. Students reserve their personal aesthetic preferences and instead channel their assessment to best serve the author's needs. Neutral questions and on-the-spot problem solving results in healthy, intentional feedback sessions.

Adjusting Their Approach: Selecting their own revision criteria bolsters participants' sense of ownership over their writing. They weigh their initial vision for the work with a more nuanced, post-workshop perspective, talking through any lingering questions with the workshop leader in conference. Ultimately, the student knows best how to meet their project goals.

Reflecting on Their Learning: Two formal artist statements—one for the workshop draft, and one for the revised draft—enable students to track the evolution of their thinking by documenting the emotional, psychological, and technical aspects of the writing process. To summarize their work and admit to its challenges is a feat in and of itself, but participants go a step further, sharing successes and outlining next steps for future drafts.

No doubt, discovery-based learning is a twenty-first-century, anti-racist approach that honors the individual's unique intellectual development. And it's so open ended! The list above is a mere glimpse of the multiple, simultaneous assessment strategies my students engage in each workshop. The point is that they look back at the end of class to marvel at their growth. That sense of awe in the face of their own power is not something that we workshop leaders can give to them. They have to give it to themselves.

Grades can't compare.

I know, I've tried.

I used to create a rubric for every one of my assignments that explicitly articulated four or five learning goals broken down into a point system. I thought this was much more equitable than simply slapping a "B" on the text, or its equivalent, the ambiguous check mark. "I'm making art transparent," I thought. After reading the student's work, I'd fill out the rubric: Solid grasp of voice, check; effective use of imagery, no check. Or maybe half credit. Tally up the points, tack on a paragraph of encouraging comments, and the student had all the insight they needed to "succeed" in future assignments. Or so I thought.

It turns out that the rubric drove my workshop participants mad. Sure, they knew what they were aiming for the next time around (I'm gonna nail imagery), but the motivation for doing so was entirely external. They'd rail at half credit especially. Why wasn't it good enough? How do I earn full credit? Their focus diverted to numbers, not words. When I'd tell them that the points didn't matter, that the purpose of the assignment was to play, risk-take, even fail, they'd hold up the rubric as evidence of my duplicity. How were they free to experiment when my point system pinned them down?

When I gave up the rubric—when I gave up authority over their work all together—I myself risked failure. Would it work? Back then, I couldn't conceive of the immensity of the gift. Because it truly is a gift, the discovery-based model, one that your workshop participants will carry with them beyond the classroom.

Wrapping Up

I schedule formal workshop late into the semester (allowing for lots of low-stakes writing exercises up top), so my class wraps rather quickly thereafter. There's time for post-workshop one-on-one conferences, in-class revision sessions, and, depending on the group, a portfolio party (in which participants physically deconstruct their Writers Notebooks, workshop drafts, and course readings with scissors and glue sticks and scribbles of "I had NO idea what voice was here! [arrow] But look now! [arrow]"). Portfolio parties are messy and loud and at their best when students point to one another, borrowing excerpts from one another's work to paste into their document ("Thanks to Carlos' poem [arrow], I was inspired to write this line! [arrow]").

At this point in the workshop, I e-mail each of my students with words of encouragement. These e-mails are about them, not their final projects. Such encouragement goes a long way in acknowledging their commitment and hard work, energizing that final creative push.

Participants go on to revise their workshop drafts, complete with accompanying artist statements. I should note that in their revision artist statements, they include suggestions for how to improve the course—suggestions that I immediately implement into future course lesson plans. When we reconvene in class, participants select portions of their revisions to read aloud—whatever they're most proud of, or whatever is most changed. We don't comment on the revisions. We just applaud the success of a second attempt.

The final assignment is a different sort of end-of-term reading. Instead of gathering to feature a select few "best" writers, we gather to celebrate our collective power. This takes the form of a brunch. Potluck style, at one of the students' apartments or else my home. A change in venue is important. We drink too much coffee and talk and eat. Eventually we settle into a circle to read to one another. The students have written letters. Kind, eloquent, personal letters in praise of their creative community. These letters are typed and proofread. Sometimes they come in the form of a song or a short film.

My prompt is simple: "What did you learn?"

Every single time I join this circle, I'm overcome with pride at workshop participants' generosity toward one another and themselves, at their vulnerability and tears and laughter, at the simplicity of their sincerity when it is so much easier to choose pretension. We listen to one another one last time with mindfulness and care. Everyone is fully present, despite feeling hungover or stressed or tired.

"We've become a team," one student wrote.

"We're artists wanting to help other artists," wrote another.

"Every single one of you inspired me to work harder," wrote a third.

Together we lean into this easy camaraderie, and I can't help but think of my colleagues, isolated in their offices, stacks of student work accumulating in boxes outside their doors, work that they dread grading despite having already determined students' ranking in the class. I know I'll have my own work to do, revisiting students' workshop artist statement, revision artist statement, and final reflective letter as a means to track the narrative of their growth over the course of the workshop, but I'll have this memory to animate their words.

Why, I wonder. Why choose the old way, when there's something so much better, truer, infinitely more human, within our grasp?

This is my offering to you, all that I've learned.

A Letter to Close

Dear Reader,

A police car parked in front of my house yesterday, blocking the driveway. My seven-year-old son watched from the window. "They can't come for us if we didn't do anything wrong, right, Daddy?" he asked. My husband, a Black man, laughed.

We needed to go to the grocery store, so my husband took a picture of the police car and posted it on Instagram, then handed me a Post-it note on which he had written the phone number of an older white male colleague. He walked away from me and toward the police officer. My body said *no, don't go, I'll go, please no*. All that long driveway, my body pulsing with *something's wrong, this is wrong*.

My son chased after him—"Wait for me, Daddy!"—and I stood outside the garage with tears in my eyes, past and present and future blurring into one.

And then it was, "Good morning, sir," and "If it's not too much trouble, sir."

"He was just doing paperwork," my son explained as we backed out of the driveway, but I was silent and my husband was silent and it was a long time before either of us said anything.

What do our bodies do with all we don't say?

Does your body suffer, too, knowing what it knows? That it's wrong. The everyday shootings. The children, caged. The blue lights and brown boys, men, dead. The endless assault by white supremacy: Power. Control. Domination.

How do we reconcile this knowledge? Do we bow our heads, swallow the scream, get on and off Facebook?

Maybe this book can teach us voice. To speak out, to speak back, to say what we know but don't allow ourselves to feel, because to do so would be equal parts pain and pardon.

Maybe this book can teach me courage, because the closer I get to finishing, the more fearful I am of its reception. I was so sure, at the beginning, that this project was my life's purpose, but now that I'm a month away from giving birth to my second son, I surprise myself by wondering, "All that ugliness, is it worth it?"

Ugliness on ugliness on death. How do we mourn racism and live racism and fight racism all at once?

Maybe this book, in committing words onto the page, is a success in and of itself. Who cares if every time I read the words aloud I cry? This is my life's work, but it's also my life story. The pedagogy is necessarily personal. I can only hope that someone, somewhere, might read it and attempt a different way, a better way, freeing our bodies to speak more and suffer less.

I am so tired. Grief-stricken and afraid.

Lend me your hope?

They say that a writer's work must stand alone, that I won't be there when you pick up my book, but maybe I can be, if you let me. Maybe we can build this thing together.

In solidarity,
Felicia

APPENDIX 1:

Platforming Writers of Color: A Twenty-First-Century Reference Guide

Together let's dispel the myth of scarcity: that there aren't any quality writers of color out there. Visit www.antiracistwork shop.com to access—and add to—an ever-evolving, multi-genre compilation of contemporary writers of color and progressive online publishing platforms. This living document is intended as a dynamic educational resource and springboard for further research. Call it recommended reading.

APPENDIX 2:

Sample Lesson Plan

For educators who are curious about the logistics of an anti-racist workshop in action, consider the following sample lesson plans for classes in early, mid-, and late term. These lesson plans are meant to serve as a starting point and are therefore purposefully open-ended.

Workshop Overview

TRADITIONAL WRITING WORKSHOP

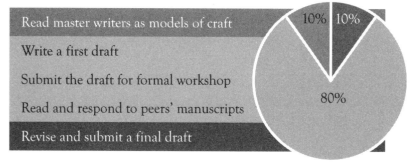

Read master writers as models of craft

Write a first draft

Submit the draft for formal workshop

Read and respond to peers' manuscripts

Revise and submit a final draft

10% 10%

80%

ANTI-RACIST WRITING WORKSHOP

Build confidence and community through daily snack, check-in, and freewriting opportunities

Participate in daily informal workshops and self-assessment opportunities

Check one's positionality and body language when engaging with another's ideas

20%

30%

30%

20%

Explore a living archive of scanned print material, sourced pdfs, and multimedia art that features people of color, women, queer, differently abled, and gender-nonconforming artists

Read for craft and then collectively define craft elements

Study how to frame effective questions and then interview contemporary writers

Read Liz Lerman and then collectively negotiate writing workshop rituals

Practice how to workshop in favor of the writer's agenda as opposed to one's personal aesthetic preferences

Prepare a pre-workshop conference agenda and then lead a meeting with the workshop leader

Write a workshop draft and artist statement

Lead a formal workshop

Lead a post-workshop conference with the workshop leader

Revise the draft (both in and out of class) and write an artist statement

Craft a reflective portfolio of learning

Select an excerpt from the revised draft to read aloud

Write a reflective letter to workshop peers and share over food
and drinks

Sample Lesson Plans

EARLY WORKSHOP AGENDA

Prepare the room:

- ❖ Write the course goals at the top of board (for example, my Nonfiction Writing goals are "Confidence, Vulnerability, and Truth"; my Inspiration Lab goals are "Curiosity, Stamina, and Risk").

- ❖ Below, add a quote—ideally from a person of color—to serve as the day's thematic focal point.

- ❖ Play music—your own, or a student volunteer's.

- ❖ Spray aromatherapy room mist.

- ❖ Arrange tables and chairs into one large circle or smaller clusters of four or five.

Greet students by name as they arrive.

Collectively applaud the student who brought snack.

Share snack and commence check-in.

Deliver a microlecture on an element of the creative process (for example, exercising vulnerability).

Pair the lecture with one or more freewriting exercises that touch on students' personal writing journeys. Students write by hand in their writer's notebook.

Convene to collectively survey our body language.

Students stand and read excerpts from their freewrites aloud while classmates listen attentively.

Break

Present a short interactive lesson on the thematic focal point. Interweave discussion and incorporate a multimedia element that features another voice besides your own—for example, a short excerpt from a podcast or interview—ideally one that features people of color, women, queer, differently abled, and/or gender-nonconforming artists.

Lead a quick writing exercise that bridges the lesson and the homework assignment. Students write by hand in their writer's notebook.

Provide an overview of the homework assignment, then an opportunity for questions.

MID-WORKSHOP AGENDA

Prepare the room:

✧ Write the course goals at the top of board (for example, my Nonfiction Writing goals are "Confidence, Vulnerability, and Truth"; my Inspiration Lab goals are "Curiosity, Stamina, and Risk").

✧ Below, add a quote—ideally from a person of color—to serve as the day's thematic focal point.

✧ Play music—your own, or a student volunteer's.

✧ Spray aromatherapy room mist.

✧ Arrange tables and chairs into one large circle or smaller clusters of four or five.

Greet students by name as they arrive.

Collectively applaud the student who brought snack.

Share snack and commence check-in.

Engage in a quick freewriting exercise that touches on students' personal writing journeys: How has the writing felt? How has the editing felt?

Discuss the difference between rereading our work, editing our work, and revising our work.

Deliver a quick lecture on macro- vs. micro-editing using examples from your own writing.

Remind students that they are the first and final authority on their writing. Ask them to retrieve printed copies of their pre-workshop drafts in progress.

Lead macro-editing exercise #1: By choosing to look at our drafts from various angles, we may yield different writing that makes our discovery more enriching.

OMISSION

Reread your work with an eye for what's NOT there. Make notes
to yourself in the margins:

✧ Are there places where you are holding back? Why?

✧ Are there gaps in time that feel significant?

✧ How might you braid in the missing material?

✧ Short freewrite.

DEEPENING

✧ When you look back on your writing, pinpoint what was
easy and what was extremely difficult to put into words?

✧ This ease or discomfort may be telling and offer opportunities for deepening or expansion.

✧ Star these sections throughout your draft to pursue
tonight.

PERSPECTIVE

✧ Is your writing voice indicative of how the narrator felt in
the past (then)?

✧ If the narrator reflected back now, what has changed?
What do they see now that they couldn't see then?

✧ Circle opportunities to layer in the "now" voice in an
effort to acknowledge a shift in perspective.

✧ Short freewrite.

Break

Lead macro-editing exercise #2:

ARRANGEMENT

✧ Where do you start? Where do you end? What comes

in between, turn by turn? And WHY? With paper and colored pencils, map out your draft, remembering that arrangement creates movement and meaning.

✦ Review your map and ask yourself: What belongs? What doesn't? (Optional breakout in pairs or whole group discussion to troubleshoot.)

✦ Rereading your work, have you brainstormed any additional elements that need incorporating?

✦ Short freewrite.

Review the artist statement assignment to determine if you need clarification.

Provide an overview of the homework assignment, then an opportunity for questions.

Glance ahead to tomorrow's micro-editing session.

FORMAL WORKSHOP AGENDA

Prepare the room:

- ✧ Write the course goals at the top of board (for example, my Nonfiction Writing goals are "Confidence, Vulnerability, and Truth"; my Inspiration Lab goals are "Curiosity, Stamina, and Risk").

- ✧ Below, outline the class' adaptation of the Critical Response Process.

- ✧ Play music—your own, or a student volunteer's.

- ✧ Spray aromatherapy room mist.

- ✧ Arrange tables and chairs into one large circle.

Distribute copies of the collective workshop vocabulary by each seat as a prompt to keep the conversation craft-based. Alternately, project this language on the wall.

Writers arrive early to distribute copies of their workshop drafts by each seat. These are printed and stapled with the artist statement on page one. To ease this process, you might ask writers to e-mail their work the night before and print copies for them.

Greet participants by name as they arrive.

Collectively applaud the student who brought snack.

Share snack while silently reading writer #1's artist statement.

Writer #1 starts a timing device for thirty minutes, greets everyone, then reads their work aloud. Participants follow in real time on the page, marking with a star what moves them and marking with a question mark what confuses them.

Writer #1 moderates workshop using the Liz Lerman methodology, then thanks participants and outlines next steps.

Ask responders to record their names on writer #1's draft, then pass it forward for collection.

Lead a collective stretching exercise (if workshopping four writers) or offer a short break (if workshopping two writers).

Repeat.

Congratulate the group for their generosity and sincerity and resolve any errant behavior on the spot.

Plan to meet writers for post-workshop conferences.

END-OF-WORKSHOP AGENDA

Prepare the room:

✧ Write the course goals at the top of board (for example, my Nonfiction Writing goals are "Confidence, Vulnerability, and Truth"; my Inspiration Lab goals are "Curiosity, Stamina, and Risk").

✧ Below, add a quote—ideally from a person of color—to serve as the day's thematic focal point.

✧ Play music—your own, or a student volunteer's.

✧ Spray aromatherapy room mist.

✧ Arrange tables and chairs into one large circle or smaller clusters of four or five.

Greet students by name as they arrive.

Collectively applaud the student who brought snack.

Share snack and commence check-in.

Marvel at the group's accomplishments over the course of the workshop. List them on the board and invite students to add to it.

Lead a micro-lecture on the power of writing and being present in our own lives.

Pair the lecture with one or more freewriting exercises that touch on students' personal writing journeys. Students write by hand in their writer's notebook.

Convene to collectively survey our body language.

Students stand and read excerpts from their freewrites aloud while classmates listen attentively.

Break

Ask students to retrieve their Writer's Notebook, copies of readings that moved them, drafts of their writing, the syllabus, handouts, interview questions, etc. They will have prepared these materials in advance.

Direct them to craft an informal reflective portfolio, a visual aid that demonstrates their growth over the workshop. Guide them to be creative and introspective as they make sense of the mess of paper in front of them:

✧ Spread out. Cut things up, paste them elsewhere. Highlight. Tack on Post-it notes. White out words. Draw arrows. Tape in foldouts, pop-ups. The idea is to represent your learning over the course of the workshop.

✧ Where did you begin on your writing journey? Where are you now? Point to examples that demonstrate these changes.

✧ What inspired or influenced your writing? Where, exactly? (You're welcome to reference one another's writing. I will gladly make copies of student work.)

✧ What do you want your work to say to others about you as a writer?

✧ And how does your work achieve our course goals of Curiosity, Stamina, and Risk?

Play music, make a mess, enjoy.

ACKNOWLEDGMENTS

Two years ago, I traveled to Reykjavik, Iceland, to read a short speech about how racial bias affected my graduate school experience at the University of Iowa. I stood at the podium and openly sobbed. I'd practiced that speech over and over again, and yet in the moment, I was overcome with such intense vulnerability, like I was committing an act of betrayal for speaking my experience out loud.

There was something to that moment, that shared intimacy, that elicited an outpouring from audience members. Writers of color reached out to me afterwards to talk about their own toxic MFA programs. White ally educators wanted to know how to avoid replicating harm.

Amy Benson was one such ally. She reached out to me one year later. "I attended your panel last summer," she wrote, "and was entirely engrossed by the innovations you've made to the writing workshop. I think and think and think about it. So much so that I applied for a grant for writers who teach to dig into ways to build more inclusive, supportive and productive writing programs." Thank you, Amy Benson, for emboldening me to continue this work, and thank you to the consortium of liberal arts educators who convened at Rhodes College to strategize change.

Thank you, Colorado College, for the space and time to write.

Thank you, Ramona Lindsey and the Hadley Creative Fellows, for further advancing the project and gifting me with the courage to claim my value as an artist.

Thank you, Mia Alvarado and Catina Bacote, for your swift service as readers.

Thank you, Sultana Noormuhammad, for "getting it."

Thank you, Bonnie Sunstein, for your fixed faith in my abilities.

Thank you, Stephanie Elizondo Griest, for listening with grace. You inspire me to be a better woman.

Thank you, Heal McKnight, for modeling radical love and loyalty.

Thank you, students, for your trust.

Thank you, Maya Marshall, for your passion, patience, and careful consideration of my words, and to the Haymarket team for your support of this book.

Kevin Coval, it began with you. Humboldt Park Fieldhouse, MLK Day. You led me to Young Chicago Authors and forever changed my life.

Mariah, Christina, August: carry it forward, change the lives of others.

Jerry, I saved every one of your messages and replayed them when I needed encouragement. Brother, you are in my head and in my heart.

Dad, you lifted me up, and Mom, you held it down. Thank you for being my first and most important teachers.

Taos, when I'd log onto Facebook you'd ask, "What are your writing goals for the day, Mama?" Thank you. I couldn't have finished the book without your sweet and public shaming. Nor could I finish it without you, Idris, my love, my champion, who answered my angst with an impatient, "The book is done." And so it is.

ENDNOTES

PREFACE

1. June Jordan, "Introduction," in *June Jordan's Poetry for the People: A Revolutionary Blueprint*, ed. Lauren Muller (New York: Routledge, 1995), 5.
2. Jordan, "Introduction," 7.
3. Though it is a radical reclaiming of the historically racist label "colored people," I concede that "people of color" fails to acknowledge the physical, mental, emotional, and cultural violence specifically targeted against Black and Indigenous peoples. For the purposes of this book, I will use "people of color" to translate broadly to those racial and ethnic communities who do not benefit from white supremacy. I grant that my language falls short of total inclusivity.

INTRODUCTION: DECOLONIZING THE CREATIVE CLASSROOM

1. Junot Diaz, "MFA VS. POC," *New Yorker*, April 30, 2014, https://www.newyorker.com/books/page-turner/mfa-vs-poc.
2. Sandra Cisneros, "The House on Mango Street," interview by Leonard Lopate, *The Leonard Lopate Show*, WNYC. 93.9 FM, April 23, 2009, audio, 15:00, https://www.wnyc.org/story/58246-the-house-on-mango-street/.
3. I'm borrowing and applying this definition of anti-racism. "Anti-racism is the active process of identifying and eliminating racism by changing systems, organizational structures, policies and practices, and attitudes, so that power is redistributed and shared equitably." From, National Action Committee on the Status of Women (NAC) International Perspectives: Women and Global Solidarity. http://www.aclrc.com/antiracism-defined
4. Roxane Gay, "Where Things Stand," *Rumpus*, June 6, 2012,

196

https://therumpus.net/2012/06/where-things-stand/.

5. Audre Lorde, *Sister Outsider: Essays & Speeches* (Berkeley: Crossing Press, 2007), 103.

CHAPTER 1: PREPARING FOR CHANGE

1. Sam Levin, "'They Don't Belong': Police Called on Native American Teens on College Tour," *Guardian*, May 4, 2018, https://www.theguardian.com /us-news/2018/may/04/native-american-students-colorado-state-college -tour-police.

2. Dialynn Dwyer, "'I Am Not a Threat': Smith College Student Says She's 'Terrified' to Return to Campus after Having Police Called on Her," *Boston Globe*, August 23, 2018, https://www.boston.com/news/local-news/2018 /08/23/smith-college-student-oumou-kanoute-reflects-on-returning-to -campus-after-police-called.

3. Cleve R. Wootson, "A Black Yale Student Fell Asleep in Her Dorm's Common Room. A White Student Called Police," *Washington Post*, May 11, 2018, https://www.washingtonpost.com/news/grade-point/wp/2018/05/10/a -black-yale-student-fell-asleep-in-her-dorms-common-room-a-white-student -called-police/?noredirect=on&utm_term=.4c7ee9a5a6b9.

4. Travis Anderson, "Longtime UMass Amherst Worker Says He Is 'Stressed Out' by Racial Profiling Incident," *Boston Globe*, September 17, 2018, https://www .bostonglobe.com/metro/2018/09/17/police-called-black-umass-amherst -employee-walking-work/0UIHhb69tMQIPL9dPx2DqL/story.html.

5. George Yancy, "The Ugly Truth of Being a Black Professor in America," *Chronicle of Higher Education*, April 29, 2018, https://www.chronicle.com /article/The-Ugly-Truth-of-Being-a/243234.

6. Kiese Laymon, *Heavy: An American Memoir* (New York: Scribner, 2018), 71–72.

7. Claudia Rankine, "In Our Way: Racism in Creative Writing," *Writer's Chronicle* 49, no. 2 (Oct/Nov 2016): 50.

8. Toni Morrison, *Playing in the Dark: Whiteness and the Literary Imagination* (New York: Vintage Books: 1993), 5.

9. David Mura, "Ferguson, Whiteness as Default, and the Teaching of Creative Writing," *Writer's Chronicle* 49, no. 2 (Oct/Nov 2016): 39–40.

10. Peter Elbow, *Writing with Power: Techniques for Mastering the Writing Process* (New York: Oxford University Press, 1998), 16.

11. Inspired by Austin Kleon, *Steal Like an Artist: 10 Things Nobody Told You about Being Creative* (New York: Workman Publishing Company, 2012).

12. Lynda Barry, *What It Is* (Singapore: Drawn & Quarterly, 2008), 8.

13. Barry, *What It Is*, 135.

14. Lisa Lee, "Racial Invisibility and Erasure in the Writing Workshop," *VIDA:*

Women in Literary Arts, January 11, 2016, http://www.vidaweb.org/report -from-the-field-racial-invisibility-and-erasure-in-the-writing-workshop/.

15. Chris Stark, "Crazy," in *How Dare We! Write: A Multicultural Creative Writing Discourse*, ed. Sherry Quan Lee (Ann Arbor: Modern History Press, 2017), 51–52.

16. Peter Elbow, *Vernacular Eloquence: What Speech Can Bring to Writing* (New York: Oxford University Press, 2012), cover copy.

17. bell hooks, *Teaching to Transgress: Education as the Practice of Freedom* (New York: Routledge, 1994), 43.

18. Robin Diangelo, *White Fragility: Why It's So Hard for White People to Talk about Racism* (Boston: Beacon Press, 2018), 14.

19. De-canon: A Visibility Project is a "pop-up library" and web resource project that showcases literary art by writers/artists of color. Our goal is to put forth an alternative literary "canon"—or multiple canons—that are inclusive, diverse, and multi-storied in their approach to representation. De-canon wishes to challenge existing ideas of what constitutes the North American literary canon, especially in our current culture. https://www.de-canon.com/.

20. Kathy Luckett and Shannon Morreira, "Questions Academics Can Ask to Decolonise Their Classrooms." *The Conversation*, October 17, 2018, https://theconversation.com/questions-academics-can-ask-to-decolonise-their -classrooms-103251.

CHAPTER 2: FOSTERING ENGAGEMENT, MINDFULNESS, AND GENEROSITY

1. Paulo Freire, *Pedagogy of the Oppressed* (New York: Bloomsbury, 2000), 72.

2. Freire, *Pedagogy of the Oppressed*, 76.

3. Freire, *Pedagogy of the Oppressed*, 75.

4. Freire, *Pedagogy of the Oppressed*, 92–93.

5. bell hooks, *Teaching to Transgress: Education as the Practice of Freedom* (New York: Routledge, 1994), 40–41.

6. It's important to note that the majority of the students that I work with are able-bodied and therefore my language is biased. I recognize this as a personal blind spot and invite you to adapt practices that accommodate your students' individual needs.

7. Gloria Anzaldúa, "Speaking in Tongues: A Letter to Third World Women Writers," in *This Bridge Called My Back: Writings by Radical Women of Color*, eds. Gloria Anzaldúa and Cherríe Moraga (Albany: SUNY Press, 2015), 164.

8. Anzaldúa, "Speaking in Tongues: A Letter to Third World Women Writers," 167.

9. Thích Nhất Hạnh, *The Art of Communicating* (New York: Harper Collins, 2013), 15.

10. Lynda Barry, *Syllabus: Notes from an Accidental Professor* (New York: Drawn and Quarterly, 2014), 4.

11. Hạnh, *The Art of Communicating*, 51.

12. Bonnie Friedman, *Writing Past Dark: Envy, Fear, Distraction, and Other Dilemmas in the Writer's Life* (New York: Harper Perennial, 2014), preface, Kindle.

13. Tanaya Winder, "Fiercely Embrace Ancestral Resilience," Facebook, February 13, 2019, https://www.facebook.com/tanaya.winder/posts/10104475968749543.

CHAPTER 3: INSTITUTING READING AND WRITING RITUALS

1. Donna Kate Rushin, "The Bridge Poem," in *This Bridge Called My Back: Writings by Radical Women of Color*, eds. Gloria Anzaldúa and Cherríe Moraga (Albany: SUNY Press, 2015), xxxiii–xxxiv.

2. Peter Elbow, *Writing with Power: Techniques for Mastering the Writing Process* (New York: Oxford University Press, 1998), 15.

3. Elbow, *Writing with Power*, 18.

4. Austin Kleon, *Steal Like an Artist: 10 Things Nobody Told You about Being Creative* (New York: Workman Publishing Company, 2012), 50.

5. Kleon, *Steal Like an Artist*, 54.

6. Anne Lamott, *Bird by Bird: Some Instructions on Writing and Life* (New York: Anchor Books, 1995), 32.

7. Elbow, *Writing with Power*, 14.

8. Inspired by Austin Kleon's creative guidebook *Steal Like an Artist*.

9. Julia Cameron, *The Right to Write: An Invitation and Initiation into the Writing Life* (New York: Tarcher/Putnam, 1998), 155.

10. Gretchen Rubin, "Harnessing the Power of Frequency," in *Manage Your Day-To-Day: Build Your Routine, Find Your Focus, and Sharpen Your Creative Mind*, ed. Jocelyn K. Glei (Las Vegas: Amazon Publishing, 2013), 33.

11. Rubin, "Harnessing the Power of Frequency," 35.

12. Elbow, *Writing with Power*, 32.

13. Susan Bell, *The Artful Edit: On the Practice of Editing Yourself* (New York: W. W. Norton & Co., 2007), 2.

14. Elbow, *Writing with Power*, 145.

15. Shampa Biswas, "Advice on Advising: How to Mentor Minority Students," *ChronicleVitae*, March 13, 2019, https://chroniclevitae.com/news/2172-advice-on-advising-how-to-mentor-minority-students?cid=VTEVPMSED1.

16. Shampa Biswas, "Advice on Advising: How to Mentor Minority Students."

CHAPTER 4: COMPLETING THE CANON

1. Claudia Rankine, "In Our Way: Racism in Creative Writing," *The Writer's Chronicle* 49, no. 2 (Oct/Nov 2016): 50.

2. Joseph Epstein, "The Style of Genius," *Literary Genius: 25 Classic Writers Who Define English and American Literature*, ed. Joseph Epstein (Philadelphia: Paul Dry Books, 2007), 4.

3. Rankine, "In Our Way: Racism in Creative Writing," 50.

4. Austin Channing Brown, *I'm Still Here: Black Dignity in a World Made for Whiteness* (New York: Convergent Books, 2018), 21.

5. Fred D'Aguiar, "Toward a New Creative Writing Pedagogy," *The Writer's Chronicle* 49, no. 2 (Oct/Nov 2016): 90.

6. KC Trommer, "How Do We Fix the MFA? Toward A Better Creative Writing Degree," LitHub, September 12, 2016, https://lithub.com/how-do-we-fix-the-mfa/.

7. D'Aguiar, "Toward a New Creative Writing Pedagogy," 90.

8. DeRay Mckesson, *On the Other Side of Freedom: The Case for Hope* (New York: Viking Press, 2018), 92–93.

9. Mckesson argues against the white ally, who "is not willing to risk anything besides her mental comfort," and for the white accomplice, who "faces her own participation in whiteness, acknowledges it, and then looks beyond that personal acknowledgment to identify how her awareness can be applied to changing the system and mind-sets that prop up the system." *On the Other Side of Freedom: The Case for Hope*, 101.

10. Mckesson, *On the Other Side of Freedom: The Case for Hope*, 88.

11. Cherríe Moraga, "Catching Fire," *This Bridge Called My Back: Writings by Radical Women of Color*, eds. Cherríe Moraga and Gloria Anzaldúa (New York: SUNY Press, 2015), xxiv.

12. Beth Nguyen, "Unsilencing the Writer's Workshop," Lit Hub, April 3, 2019, https://lithub.com/unsilencing-the-writing-workshop/.

13. Toni Morrison, *Playing in the Dark: Whiteness and the Literary Imagination* (New York: Vintage Books: 1993), 8.

CHAPTER 5: OWNING THE LANGUAGE OF CRAFT

1. Austin Channing Brown, *I'm Still Here: Black Dignity in a World Made for Whiteness* (New York: Convergent Books, 2018), 52–53.

2. bell hooks, *Teaching to Transgress: Education as the Practice of Freedom* (New York: Routledge, 1994), 41.

3. David Mura, "Ferguson, Whiteness as Default, and the Teaching of Creative Writing," *The Writer's Chronicle* 49, no. 2 (Oct/Nov 2016): 39–40.

4. David Mura, *A Stranger's Journey: Race, Identity, and Narrative Craft in Writing*

(Athens: University of Georgia Press, 2018), 4.

5.   Mura, *A Stranger's Journey*, 25.

6.   1970s Aboriginal activist group slogan originating from Queensland, Australia.

CHAPTER 6: TEACHING WRITERS TO WORKSHOP

1.   Eboo Patel, *Acts of Faith: The Story of an American Muslim, the Struggle for the Soul of a Generation* (Boston: Beacon Press, 2007), xvii.

2.   Eboo Patel, "Eboo Patel on James Baldwin's 'Autobiographical Notes,'" Beacon Broadside, June 28, 2013, https://www.beaconbroadside.com /broadside/2013/06/eboo-patel-on-james-baldwin.html.

3.   Liz Lerman and John Borstel, *Liz Lerman's Critical Response Process: A Method for Getting Useful Feedback on Anything You Make, from Dance to Dessert* (Takoma Park: Dance Exchange, 2003), 6.

4.   Lerman and Borstel, *Liz Lerman's Critical Response Process*, 6.

5.   Lerman and Borstel, *Liz Lerman's Critical Response Process*, 19.

6.   Lerman and Borstel, *Liz Lerman's Critical Response Process*, 20.

7.   Lerman and Borstel, *Liz Lerman's Critical Response Process*, 21.

8.   Lerman and Borstel, *Liz Lerman's Critical Response Process*, 22.

9.   Patel, *Acts of Faith*, 179.

10. Beverly Daniel Tatum, *"Why Are All the Black Kids Sitting Together in the Cafeteria?" And Other Conversations about Race* (New York: Basic Books, 1999), 11–12.

CHAPTER 7: CONFERENCING AS CRITIQUE

1.   Cornel Pewewardy, "Culturally Responsible Pedagogy in Action: An American Indian Magnet School," In *Teaching Diverse Populations: Formulating A Knowledge Base*, eds. E. Hollins, J. King, and W. Hayman (Albany: State University of New York Press, 1993), 77–92.

CHAPTER 8: PROMOTING CAMARADERIE AND COLLECTIVE POWER

1.   Amairani Alamillo and Han Sayles, "Diversify the Curriculum," https:// www.change.org/p/faculty-of-colorado-college-diversify-the-curriculum.

2.   "Boycott English," https://sites.google.com/view/boycottwilliamsenglish/home.

3.   "Concerning white nationalism on the University of Nevada, Reno campus," October 7, 2019, https://docs.google.com/forms/d/e/1FAIpQLScM7R _Jj-I1pIy2ZK0mwFgUUN2ffkr56MM8btROoHiVfRo9lg/viewform.

4.   "An Open Letter to the Yale Administration from Black Graduate Students and Allies," *Conversation X*, May 26, 2018, http://www.conversationx.com

/2018/05/26/an-open-letter-to-the-yale-administration-from-black-graduate
-students-and-allies/.

5.   "Open Letter to F&M Concerning Incidents of Racism, Need for Change
in Administration, Steps That Must Be Taken," *College Reporter*, December
9, 2019, https://www.the-college-reporter.com/2019/11/10/open-letter
-to-fm-concerning-incidents-of-racism-need-for-change-in-administration
-steps-that-can-be-taken/.

6.   Jill Tiefenthaler, "Provide Input on Campus Antiracism Plan," August 27
2019, https://www.coloradocollege.edu/offices/presidentsoffice/pres
-announcement/provide-input-on-antiracism-initiative-plan.html?com
.dotmarketing.htmlpage.language=1&host_id=e19a1071-63ad-45c4-a9b1
-0f5cd4869309.

7.   Derald Wing Sue, "An Open Letter to Brothers and Sisters of Color,"
https://www.tc.columbia.edu/diversity/about-our-office/open-letter-to
-brothers-and-sisters-of-color/.

8.   Priya Parker, *The Art of Gathering: How We Meet and Why It Matters* (New
York: Riverhead Books, 2018), 16.

About the Author

Photo by Idris Goodwin

Felicia Rose Chavez is an award-winning educator with an MFA in Creative Nonfiction from the University of Iowa. She is the author of *The Anti-Racist Writing Workshop: How to Decolonize the Creative Classroom* and coeditor of *The BreakBeat Poets Volume 4: LatiNEXT* with Willie Perdomo and José Olivarez. Chavez served as Program Director to Young Chicago Authors and founded GirlSpeak, a literary webzine for young women. She went on to teach writing at the University of New Mexico, where she was distinguished as the Most Innovative Instructor of the Year, the University of Iowa, where she was distinguished as the Outstanding Instructor of the Year, and Colorado College, where she received the Theodore Roosevelt Collins Outstanding Faculty Award. Her creative scholarship earned her a Ronald E. McNair Fellowship, a University of Iowa Graduate Dean's Fellowship, a Riley Scholar Fellowship, and a Hadley Creatives Fellowship. Originally from Albuquerque, New Mexico, Felicia currently serves as Scholar-in-Residence in Creativity and Innovation at Colorado College. Find her at www.antiracistworkshop.com.

About Haymarket Books

Haymarket Books is a radical, independent, nonprofit book publisher based in Chicago.

Our mission is to publish books that contribute to struggles for social and economic justice. We strive to make our books a vibrant and organic part of social movements and the education and development of a critical, engaged, international left.

We take inspiration and courage from our namesakes, the Haymarket martyrs, who gave their lives fighting for a better world. Their 1886 struggle for the eight-hour day—which gave us May Day, the international workers' holiday—reminds workers around the world that ordinary people can organize and struggle for their own liberation. These struggles continue today across the globe—struggles against oppression, exploitation, poverty, and war.

Since our founding in 2001, Haymarket Books has published more than five hundred titles. Radically independent, we seek to drive a wedge into the risk-averse world of corporate book publishing. Our authors include Noam Chomsky, Arundhati Roy, Rebecca Solnit, Angela Y. Davis, Howard Zinn, Amy Goodman, Wallace Shawn, Mike Davis, Winona LaDuke, Ilan Pappé, Richard Wolff, Dave Zirin, Keeanga-Yamahtta Taylor, Nick Turse, Dahr Jamail, David Barsamian, Elizabeth Laird, Amira Hass, Mark Steel, Avi Lewis, Naomi Klein, and Neil Davidson. We are also the trade publishers of the acclaimed Historical Materialism Book Series and of Dispatch Books.

Also Available from Haymarket Books

Black Lives Matter at School
Edited by Jesse Hagopian and Denisha Jones

Freedom Is a Constant Struggle: Ferguson, Palestine, and the Foundations of a Movement
Angela Y. Davis, edited by Frank Barat, preface by Cornel West

Things That Make White People Uncomfortable
Michael Bennett and Dave Zirin